HELL

NO

WE WON'T

GO

HELL

NO

VIETNAM DRAFT RESISTERS IN CANADA

WE WON'T

Alan Haig-Brown

Foreword by Pierre Berton

RAINCOAST BOOKS
Vancouver

First published in 1996 by

Raincoast Book Distribution Ltd.
8680 Cambie Street
Vancouver, B.C.
v6p 6m9
(604) 323-7100

1 3 5 7 9 10 8 6 4 2

CANADIAN CATALOGUING IN PUBLICATION DATA

Haig-Brown, Alan, 1941-
Hell no, we won't go

ISBN 1-55192-011-5

1. Americans – Canada – Biography. 2. Vietnamese Conflict, 1961-1975 –
Draft resisters – United States – Biography. 3. Vietnamese Conflict, 1961-1975 – Desertions –
United States – Biography. 4. Immigrants – Canada – Biography. I. Title.

FC106.A5H34 1996   971'.00413'0922   C95-911101-8
F1035.A5H34 1996

All photographs by Alan Haig-Brown except for the following:
Fred Reed (Bernard Lambert); Gerald Wiviott.

Grateful acknowledgement is made to the following for
permission to reprint previously published material:

Richard Lemm: extract from "Before the Revolution" in *Prelude to the Bacchanal* (Ragweed,
1990) and extract from "To an Old Socialist." Reprinted by permission of the author.

Country Joe McDonald: lyrics to "I-Feel-Like-I'm-Fixin'-to-Die Rag."
Reprinted by permission of Alkatraz Corner Music Company.

Norm Sibum: extracts from "Export A's" in *Small Commerce* (Caitlin Press, 1978).
Reprinted by permission of the author.

Designed by Dean Allen
Project Editor: Michael Carroll
Copy Editor: Rachelle Kanefsky
Cover Photography: Lorne Bridgman

Printed and bound in Canada

To my sister Celia Haig-Brown for her listening

CONTENTS

FOREWORD

CANADA IS AN immigrant country. All who live here came from somewhere else – or their forebears did. They chose this country for a variety of reasons, but mostly they came here to get away from someplace else. And that goes back to the days of the aborigines who crossed the Bering land bridge aeons ago.

The young men who came to Canada in the sixties and seventies to avoid the American draft were excoriated by many of their fellows as cowards, afraid to fight for their country. The truth is that their decision was an act of considerable bravery. We realize now how foolish and stupid the Vietnam War was. But to defy the temper of the times took courage of a high order.

It is not easy to tear up one's roots, to leave home, family, and friends, and to become a citizen of a foreign country, even one where language is not a problem. I am reminded of the Eastern Europeans who suffered untold privations in order to leave their villages and set out for this promised land, knowing that they would never again see their blood relations.

Canada has profited from the great immigrant waves that have always matched our periods of prosperity. It is simply not true that immigrants "take jobs." In fact, they make jobs. It is to the credit of this country that we accepted the American draft resisters in spite of pressure from the United States and in spite of efforts by some of our own authorities to send them back. That they have enriched our culture goes without saying.

In earlier immigrant booms we welcomed farmers, artisans, railway builders, and construction workers. During the Vietnam War we also benefitted from actors, poets, educators, writers, social workers, musicians, publishers, and urban planners. Most of all we got people who had social consciences that they refused to betray.

Canada is immeasurably in their debt.

PIERRE BERTON
KLEINBURG, ONTARIO

ACKNOWLEDGEMENTS

A BOOK OF PROFILES obviously owes much to those who have given their time to be interviewed and to review that which has been written about them. A book, such as this one, that digs deep into people's pasts also makes emotional demands. To the 20 who gave the interviews, I owe it all, but I also want to thank those spouses and families who patiently waited out the often long hours of tape recording.

My old friend Stan Triggs arranged much of my travel in eastern Canada and gave me good company on a wonderful drive from Halifax to Montreal. In Toronto my niece Charlotte Livingstone gave me much appreciated bed and breakfast. At home in New Westminster my four children – William, James, Helen, and Linda – endured the writer's long hours and irregular moods.

At Raincoast both this book and I owe much to the careful and sensitive editing of Michael Carroll and Rachelle Kanefsky. Dean Allen's cover design answered a dilemma in a most pleasing manner that carries through to the total design. And without publisher Mark Stanton's initial and continued support this book would have neither beginning nor end.

To all of these and to my friends who have suggested other friends who might belong in the book, I offer my thanks.

Come on all of you big strong men,
Uncle Sam needs your help again;
He's got himself in a terrible jam,
Way down yonder in Vietnam;
So put down your books and pick up a gun,
We're gonna have a whole lot of fun!

And it's one, two, three,
What are we fighting for?
Don't ask me, I don't give a damn,
Next stop is Vietnam;
And it's five, six, seven,
Open up the pearly gates;
There ain't no time to wonder why,
Whoopie – we're all gonna die.

Come on, generals, let's move fast,
Your big chance has come at last;
Now you can go out and get those Reds,
The only good Commie is one that's dead;
You know that peace can only be won,
When we've blown 'em all to kingdom come!

Come on, Wall Street, don't be slow,
Why, man, this is war Au-go-go;
There's plenty good money to be made,
Supplying the army with tools of the trade;
Just hope and pray if they drop the Bomb,
They drop it on the Viet Cong!

Come on, mothers, throughout the land,
Pack your boys off to Vietnam;
Come on, fathers, don't hesitate,
Send your sons off before it's too late;
You can be the first one on your block
To have your boy come home in a box.

– COUNTRY JOE MCDONALD,
"I-FEEL-LIKE-I'M-FIXIN'-TO-DIE RAG"

INTRODUCTION

As I was finishing up this book, a television producer from Sweden, who was beginning work on a documentary with a similar theme, contacted me and asked, "How come you're interested in this subject?"

He wasn't the first to ask and I suppose I have answered somewhat differently each time, depending on my thoughts that day. There is the standard line of historians that says we must know something of where we came from to understand where we are going. But, for Canadians, that doesn't necessarily address why this particular piece of history deserves examination. So then I have to look to my own life for a clue. I was born in November 1941 in Campbell River, British Columbia, to immigrant parents. My father was from England and my mother had come from the United States. In fact, I was baptized on December 7, Pearl Harbor Day, the same day that one of my uncles was reported missing, erroneously as it turned out, in action on the U.S. Navy battleship *Arizona*. My grandfather and namesake, Lieutenant Colonel Alan Haig-Brown, had been killed in the Great War, while my father, Roderick Haig-Brown, served in the Second World War. One of my earliest memories is of his homecoming.

Much later I well remember the Cuban missile crisis of 1962. Having been a high school dropout, I returned to an adult school for grade 12. That morning, when the radio news told us that Soviet and

American leaders were poised with their fingers over the red buttons of Armageddon, a number of us sat in the school cafeteria and talked about what we would do if we were called to fight. Most of us, myself included, would have lined up and gotten on the bus to the recruiting centre, not because we had any illusions about the glory of nuclear war, but because we believed that it was obviously our turn to do that which our grandfathers and fathers had done without question.

I remind myself of this so that I can appreciate what the Vietnam era did for those who were just a little younger than I, for those who had a little space between themselves and the glorification of World War II that I had been raised with. A decade after the Cuban missile crisis there was no longer the remotest possibility that a group of 20-year-olds would sit in a college cafeteria with the same unquestioning acceptance that my friends and I thought nothing of in 1962. A complete transformation had occurred so that young people had come to challenge the unflinching, patriotic embracement of war that is so celebrated in Tennyson's *The Charge of the Light Brigade,* the poem that contains the refrain "Into the valley of Death / Rode the six hundred."

I am a little older than most of the people I have interviewed for this book. I belong to the generation of Canadians for whom the first awareness of the American draft came on that fateful day when our musical hero, Elvis Presley, had his long hair shorn and was whisked off to Germany. He wouldn't return for two long years and would never make another good rock and roll song. When I grew my hair a little long in 1962 and went back to Campbell River on Vancouver Island to work on the commercial fishing boat that would pay my way to university the following winter, I wasn't yet called a hippie; the term *beatnik* was probably more appropriate, although I wouldn't have qualified as a true Jack Kerouac fan. When my young wife and I went hitchhiking around British Columbia with a little cardboard sign naming our destination, people picked us up and commented on how unusual it was to see a woman hitchhiking.

By the time the war evaders were arriving by the thousands in 1967, the roads of British Columbia were full of hitchhikers and I had gone north to teach in the Chilcotin country. In fact, I was teaching near Chilco Ranch in 1969 when the ranch hired a draft dodger to take care of irrigation in its hay field. With his Southern California knowledge of such matters, the draft dodger soon changed the ranch's big fields over from a simple ditch-flood system to a mechanized wheel-line sprinkler system and got record hay crops. Ironically the draft dodger later went on to develop market gardens as a replacement for food that local supermarkets imported from California. I never knew the man well, but I felt that our country lost a good person when I heard some years later that he had gone down to the coast to work on a commercial fishing boat to raise money to buy his own land and was lost at sea.

Although I was living a rather isolated life in the Chilcotin country in the late 1960s and early 1970s, I knew that things in the world outside were changing, because my long hair no longer tagged me as a beatnik. According to no less an authority than *Rolling Stone,* in a January 1972 article about police brutality in the Chilcotin in which I had been a bit player, I had become "Alexis Creek's hippie by default."

It was also while I was teaching in the Chilcotin that I met one of the most successful draft evaders and back-to-the-landers in British Columbia. "Chendi" had earned his Chilcotin name, which means "pine tree," by learning to survive in a land where winter temperatures commonly dip to 40 degrees below zero. Said to be the son of a Philadelphia lawyer, he continues to live in that beautiful but hard land after more than a quarter of a century.

In May 1995 I drove several hundred miles to visit him at his idyllic lakeside cabin. To get to his place I had to walk the last mile. The first gentle shades of green were just brushing the aspen along the trail, and high on the mountainside a spray of white blossoms marked the arrival of the mountain potato season. Near Chendi's cabin the dirt of the mountain trail displayed his bare footprint, but he was nowhere to be seen. He did answer the note I left, though, saying that he had been digging for the succulent mountain tubers and was sorry he had missed me. Sadly I never did manage to interview him for this book, which is too bad. There are still a number of men like Chendi, particularly in British Columbia, who have gone their own way and found their own kind of peace in nature's theatre. I have heard tell of another one named Rivermouth Mike on the west coast of Vancouver Island.

When I moved to Vancouver in the 1980s, I seemed to run into people constantly who were doing interesting things and who responded to questions about their youth with something like, "Well, I came up from San Francisco in '68." Not only were these people doing interesting things, but they were making real contributions to their adopted land. I met them in academic circles, in the arts, in business, and in areas of social change. I had written a book honouring the contributions to the commercial fishing industry of people from such far-flung places as Japan and Croatia, but here was a group of unique refugees from our big neighbour to the south.

I wondered how those few who had come to Canada as draft evaders or deserters – estimates range from 10,000 to 100,000 – separated themselves from the much larger number who went to Vietnam. As Myra MacPherson writes in *Long Time Passing: Vietnam and the Haunted Generation,* "Of the approximately 9 million Vietnam-era veterans, 42 percent – or 3.78 million – served in the war zone during the eleven years of United States participation. The war zone is defined as Vietnam, Laos, Cambodia, and adjacent sea and air space." And, as we all know now, more than 58,000 Americans and countless millions of Vietnamese perished.

What led to the shift in attitude among the youth of America between the Cuban missile crisis and the near-total rejection of militarism a decade later? As a parent, I wondered what kind of parenting had given those few the courage to say no. What I found when I started interviewing people was that if they have anything in common, it is a determined individualism that still recognizes community responsibility.

Some of the people with whom I spoke had celebrated love and peace along with a few grams of herbal and chemical hallucinogens, but many had been far removed from that world. The peace movement did not, it seems to me, grow out of Haight-Ashbury. Instead it grew out of careful examination by young people of the words and ideals of a powerful nation that taught its youth to think but had a great deal of difficulty accepting what they thought. Perhaps this is the principal commonality that one can extract from the wonderfully diverse people with whom I spoke for this book. And it offers a lesson that I take personally as I strive to understand my own children's concerns, a lesson, I believe, that both Canadians and Americans must appreciate in the future.

In this book I have taken many hours of taped interviews and found what I consider to be defining words from each of 20 individuals, people who have been extraordinarily patient and generous in the sharing of their personal experiences. Revisiting old pain is never easy, and many of these people even surprised themselves at how tender the wounds still are. Only one, Ruth Anderson, chose, for obvious reasons, not to use her real name. For many others who were asked to be part of this book, some of whom are well-known to the Canadian public, silence, not anonymity, may have seemed the best protection from past grief.

Not all of the 20 profiled here evaded the draft. Some, including two women, came to Canada because their consciences wouldn't allow them to stay in the United States while it waged war on peasants half a world away. Others did go to Vietnam and came to Canada on their return. Still others became part of the war machine and then opted out. Collectively the people you will meet in these pages present a unique chronicle of their times.

Like most, I have watched some of the movies that Americans have made about Vietnam. One of the people in this book, Gerald Wiviott, actually went to Vietnam, and he told me that many of the films are technically accurate in their detail but only the surrealistic

Apocalypse Now comes close to portraying the real horror. Most of the American movies (and now there are quite a few Vietnamese ones, too) are interesting for what they reveal about the American public's need to deal with its Vietnamese military defeat. They are also valuable for what they tell us about an era in which a few dissidents grew to become an overwhelming tide of youth chanting, "Hell no, we won't go!"

Since that time the military-industrial complex has never been the same, or has it? The very fact that one has to ask that question points to another important reason for this book. While it is nice to sit and reminisce about our youth, it is even more important to give today's youth and the youth of the future a record of the sometimes brave and often naive era that was the sixties. This book is for those young people of the present, and the future, who will have to make their own ethical decisions. May they do it with the conviction and commitment of the young Americans who left family and nation to come to a new land.

MICHAEL WARSH

Man with a Conscience

THE DIMINUTIVE WOMAN took her seat in the University of British Columbia meeting room, and her rich brown skin glowed in the summer sunlight streaming through a window. It was the mid-1970s and awareness of North American aboriginal issues was growing rapidly. Now a group of teachers and academics had gathered to plan a conference on First Nations education. Introductions were exchanged by the half dozen or so people at the table, and when it was the woman's turn, she introduced herself as Kau'i Warsh and added, "Well, this looks like another conference being planned for Indian women by white men."

No doubt the good liberal white men at the table experienced a range of reactions to the comment, but for everyone there it certainly served as a harbinger of the reemergence of aboriginal governments over the next 20 years. The First Nations woman who made the comment would make her contributions to this evolution with strengths that she brought from her tribal family at home in Hawaii. Many Kanakas, as native Hawaiians are called in British Columbia, had come to work and often to stay among B.C. First Nations in the 19th century when the Hudson's Bay Company controlled colonial commerce.

But Kau'i Keliipio came to British Columbia for love, not commerce. Originally she left Hawaii for Arizona, where she worked in black migrant labour communities for VISTA (the domestic U.S. Peace Corps). Later she went on to study at the University of California at Berkeley, paying her board by caring for a professor's children. At Berkeley she met and fell in love with Michael Warsh, a Southern California student and surfer. However, Michael was more than a good-time student/surfer. In fact, he had grown up with a heightened political awareness and was "a red diaper baby," as he says about his upbringing.

His grandfather, Sam, a member of the Socialist Workers' Party, immigrated to New York from Poland in 1907 and became a union activist. Michael's grandmother, Rebecca, was born into a well-to-do Warsaw lumber merchant's family and met Sam before he left Poland. She later persuaded her father to let her travel to America to visit relatives. Arriving in New York, she advertised in a Jewish newspaper to find her man. Reunited, they cashed in her return ticket. It was a loosely kept family secret that, as anarchists and atheists, they never actually married. In the 1920s the young couple moved briefly to Calgary, Alberta, and then, in 1927, with three children, to Southern California. One of the children, a son named Herman, was 16 when the United States entered World War II in 1941. Soon after, Herman married Michael's mother, Lorraine, and then enlisted in the U.S. Navy.

After the war, Herman took advantage of the GI Bill to complete a bachelor of arts in two years by attending two colleges simultaneously. He then finished a master's degree and began teaching high school history. Michael's mother's family, who were organizers with the International Garment Workers Union in Chicago, had moved out to Los Angeles after the 1929 stock market crash put so many people out of work. A trained nurse, she worked outside of the home, supporting the family while her husband attended university.

In the 1950s, while Southern California was riddled with the rot of McCarthyism, Michael grew up in a home that understood its implications. When actor Henry Fonda was blacklisted for "un-American activities," Michael's grandmother, who had attended the University of Warsaw, taught Michael about the dangers of ideologues like Senator Joseph McCarthy. The family supported the Democratic presidential and vice presidential candidacy of Adlai Stevenson and Estes Kefauver in 1956. Michael worked with young Democrats on John F. Kennedy's 1960 election campaign, but the family was skeptical about JFK's 1962 showdown over Soviet missiles in Cuba. "We talked about the irony of the U.S. having 30 or 40 military bases in Turkey and Iran with missiles pointed right at the heart of the Soviet Union, and when we have one 90 miles away, we go crazy."

In 1963 Michael graduated from high school and entered El Camino Junior College. Hanging out at Bing Copeland's surfboard shop in Redondo Beach since high school, he had become an accomplished surfer before the 1960s fad really took off. Surfing and political interests, such as the progress of the Civil Rights Movement in the American South, didn't leave a lot of time for school. When military recruiters came to the El Camino campus, he and a few others picketed. Several ex-Marines were upset with the "hippie bums" and a debate ensued.

"I was politically aware but at the same time totally naive," Michael says of that incident. "I had a lot of the rhetoric and knew a lot of statistics. We talked about the percentage of people in the United States that were black compared to the percentage in the army and the percentage that would die in the front line. I knew all kinds of things to demonstrate the inequities of our society. Those Marines were going to stomp us. At this time we were just beginning to relate all this to Vietnam."

When Kennedy was assassinated on November 22, 1963, the nation's turmoil became the young man's, and in December he went to live with an uncle in Hawaii in search of bigger waves and independence. He had just turned 18 and it was time to file with his draft board. Michael planned to file as a conscientious objector, but his father pleaded against this course; he had seen the harm done to conscientious objectors who had spent the duration of World War II in camps and were often denied civil service jobs for life. The Vietnam War hadn't yet escalated to the point where students were being drafted, and it seemed unlikely that college students would be called up. Michael was having the usual generational difficulties with his father, but took the man's advice, anyway, and filed with his board in the usual manner.

The 1960s continued to unfold. The civil rights march on Washington, D.C., took place in 1963. The summer of 1964 brought the Gulf of Tonkin incident, which prompted the U.S. government to augment their military advisers in Vietnam with combat troops. At home the Martin Luther King-inspired and Kennedy-initiated Civil Rights Act was passed, and the radical right responded by blowing up a church full of women and children in Alabama. Within a year King was awarded the Nobel Peace Prize for his work in the Civil Rights Movement. Concurrently he was becoming increasingly involved in the anti-Vietnam War movement.

Michael had moved back to San Jose and was going to college, surfing, and playing a larger role in the antiwar movement, as well. By 1965 the number of young Americans being drafted was on the rise. Michael finally applied for conscientious objector status and was also active in the campus chapter of Students for a Democratic Society. A demonstration was planned for October 16, 1965, as part of the International Days of Protest, at which people would turn in their draft cards in protest. Like hundreds of others, Michael wore a button with the October 16 date emblazoned in bright letters. He was wearing it in San Diego when he was stopped by a policeman.

"October 16, what the hell does that mean?" asked the cop.

"Well," replied Michael, "October 16 is a national day of protest and we're all going to turn in our draft cards."

The cop was furious and berated Michael and his young friends for their evil ways. His parting comment made a lasting impression on Michael: "Well, I just hope because of your efforts it doesn't mean my son can't go to war."

Events such as this melded with the teachings of Michael's historian father about truth and fiction in American politics. "I learned a lot about propaganda. About different perceptions. I learned about the War of 1812 from the Canadian standpoint and the British standpoint, as well as the American standpoint, from my family who were trying to teach me to be a critical thinker and accept the fact that history is written as a political tool and not just as an academic activity."

Michael's grandmother, Rebecca, with her degree from the University of Warsaw, and his grandfather, Sam, with his background in the early socialist movement, lived in the family home. Because Michael's mother worked through much of his childhood, the grandparents' ideas were particularly important in shaping his ideas. "I remember," he says, "being 10 years old and asking my grandfather what dialectical materialism was."

By 1966 it had been a year since Michael's application for conscientious objector status. When word came, it wasn't good; he had been turned down. "My local draft board was located in Gardenia, California, which had a large population of fiercely patriotic Japanese-Americans. Members of the draft board had fought with a famous battalion of fighting Japanese in Europe during World War II."

The antidraft movement was gaining momentum. With newspapers like the *Berkeley Barb* and *Resist Now* encouraging the movement, especially among educated young whites, Michael appealed the draft board's decision. He had a hearing before the Justice Department in 1966 in San Francisco. Since he was active in the Quaker-founded Central Committee for Conscientious Objectors, he knew what questions he would be asked. An applicant had to declare opposition to war on either religious or philosophical grounds. Michael chose philosophical. "Much of it was just trickster stuff," he recalls. Presented with a number of hypothetical situations in which he could choose to save a person at the cost of another's life, Michael responded with other hypotheses.

He was successful in convincing the woman who headed the Justice Commission hearing that he was a conscientious objector, and she recommended him to T. Oscar Smith of the Selective Service System in Washington, D.C. Smith made final rulings on conscientious objectors. "As the story goes," says Michael, "in the particular year that my appeal went to Washington, no one on appeal was granted c o status. I was turned down and it was devastating, because I believed clearly that I was a conscientious objector. I still do believe that I'm a conscientious objector."

A whole series of devastating events continued to happen. Michael and Kau'i were living together in Hayward, California, by this time, and one night as they were sitting in bed watching the eleven o'clock news like everybody else, "We saw the coverage of Martin Luther King being shot. A few months later – same bed, same TV – we watched Bobby Kennedy get shot. We were right in the middle of this tremendous turmoil, not just for us but the whole world."

That was the spring of 1968. The anti-Vietnam War movement was gaining momentum as each evening's television news brought more images of war from Southeast Asia to American homes. Until this time Michael and Kau'i, like many other young Americans, had believed that somewhere within the United States there was justice. "But now," says Michael, "the incredible sense of personal injustice in being turned down as a conscientious objector combined with the much larger social injustice that we saw around us." Increasingly they began wondering if real justice could be found in the United States.

Kau'i was involved with a black student organization, and the young couple flirted with a Marxist study group. "We were actively examining the nature of injustice in society and trying to find some kind of solution to it," says Michael.

"At the same time we came across left-wing fascists," says Kau'i. "We saw [Black Panther] Huey Newton go from great hero to just a jerk like everybody else."

There was a lot of disillusionment. Michael's political naivety was tempered by the reality of the day. But he continued to counsel people with the Central Committee for Conscientious Objectors, and in doing so he became aware of all the options, including Canada.

He explains: "There were several options that were becoming clear. Joan Baez's husband, David Harris, had opted to go to prison. Then there was the option of going into the draft and becoming a resister or conscientious objector once you were in the army. And, finally, there was the option of leaving the country. We were flirting with all of these and talking about them romantically. David Harris's experience of being sentenced to five years in jail was not very appealing to me."

Michael's relations with his father were strained, due more to generational conflict than because of differing political views. Now he began discussing his options with his father, who regretted dissuading him from applying for conscientious objector status when he was 18. His case would have been stronger at that time than when he applied on the brink of his imminent draft. Michael, who still believed he had a role working toward social change in the United States, planned to enter the army and go to jail as a resister. His father argued that it would be better to go to Canada. Eventually they convinced each other. "By the time I called him up to say I was going to Canada," Michael recalls, "he was saying that I should go to jail."

As an educated white person with a college background, Michael realized he could have entered the army and become "a darn good first lieutenant with a clerical job and never end up in Vietnam, and that frightened me. It's almost as though I was more frightened of who I was than of Vietnam. I could have very easily adapted to the system, because I wouldn't have been picking up a gun and shooting somebody."

The same skills that would have made Michael a good first lieutenant now served him as he researched and organized his exodus to Canada. He travelled to Canada and applied to the graduate school of Simon Fraser University (SFU). The son of a second cousin in Vancouver offered him a job in his import business. Then he was accepted into graduate school, applied for landed immigrant status through the consulate in Ottawa, had a hearing in San Francisco, and took the 50-point test. By the time he arrived back at the Canadian border in July 1968, the 22-year-old immigrant was already precleared. As an extra precaution, he had cut his hair and was squeaky clean. "I remember arriving at the border and sitting down in the office next to two guys who looked just like me two days earlier."

Michael found the transition to Canada relatively easy, especially since some of his friends came up and helped him move into an apartment. They all explored the new city and then one by one left Michael alone in his new land. "There I was sitting alone in the middle of Vancouver in the middle of July and I was persona non grata in my own country."

Michael's draft notice had been mailed to him shortly after he left the United States, and he learned that he would be charged with failure to report for the draft if he ever returned. As far as he knows, he was never actually charged, although he was, and is, on the FBI's list of undesirables.

In Vancouver Michael met Dutch draft dodgers who had left their country to avoid military service, and Czech refugees who had fled their country because of its politics. Both groups talked fondly about their national cultures while railing against the politics of their respective countries. These people considered themselves political refugees yet still identified with their national cultures. Michael found the American refugees less able to make that distinction. Although he also met Americans who had left the United States because they disliked the culture of their homeland, he found that they usually related the culture to the politics. Nonetheless, in the those first months, Michael considered himself a political exile who would return to the States when, and if, the political climate changed.

Michael joined a group of his countrymen to form Americans in Exile, an organization whose members believed they weren't immigrants. They got together once a week, had potlucks, and tried to help individuals who were crossing the border and didn't have the right papers. The organization would find these newcomers places to stay and contact people at the universities who would write letters to the immigration authorities on their behalf. In April 1969 the group took part in a peace march under an Americans in Exile banner. Within a year the organization fell apart as people took up their lives in Canada. "There was a strong sense of denying one's Americanness and to stop being American. People became part of the woodwork. This has always fascinated me as other groups still saw themselves in terms of their roots."

Michael was busy completing his master's thesis, and he recalls the era as a wonderful time for support among young American expatriates and from most Canadians for draft resisters. Pierre Elliott Trudeau had just been elected prime minister, and Michael recognized the same sense of youth and vibrancy in Canada that Kennedy's election had brought in the States. These were amazing times. When Vancouver's National Harbour Board granted permission for someone to build a hotel at the entrance to Stanley Park, the power of the people saved the open space, which became All Seasons Park. Conservative Tom "Terrific" Campbell was the mayor of Vancouver. A radio show host offered to pay people to cut their hair. *The Georgia Straight* was being raided by the police constantly. It was a time of great upheaval. "But it was a much more rational turmoil than in the U.S.," says Michael, recalling the faces of the police at the demonstration against Lyndon Johnson on Nob Hill in San Francisco when police on horses chased people down the street and viciously beat them.

He understood the differences between the two nations when he learned about Sitting Bull coming to Canada after General Custer's defeat at Little Big Horn. Pursued across the border by the U.S. Army, the Sioux chief was met at the border by two Mounties. In 1971, as a protest against the U.S. invasion of Cambodia, there was a demonstration at the British Columbia-Washington Peace Arch Park border crossing. Michael recounts what happened: "Some of the 10,000 people there invaded Washington and marched through Blaine where they broke some windows. They were forced back across the border by Washington State Police in full riot gear. Then there was a pitched battle right at the border, with American sheriffs running up and trying to drag a protester back, and protesters running up and trying to fight them. Meanwhile there were four or five Mounties on the Canadian side without helmets and flashlights at their sides, walking around and telling the crowd to be quiet. When a train loaded with American cars came north across the border, the masses flowed down and started throwing rocks at the GM cars that represented an American invasion. The RCMP went down and, in nice language, told the demonstrators that they would have to stop and go home, which they did. So, on one side, you have 1,000 sheriffs, some just deputized, and on this side you have a couple of Mounties saying it's over now."

Michael found some parts of that first year in Canada difficult as he struggled with his newfound status as a minor celebrity among Canadian students, many of whom looked up to him as a leader who had made a great sacrifice. At first it was pleasant, but over time the reality of having left his family and country sunk in.

His family members, although not opposed to his move, were immersed in their own personal problems and weren't always supportive. The tide of public opinion had still not swung entirely against the war in the late sixties. Michael feels that didn't happen until the National Guard started shooting white middle-class college kids at Kent State in 1970. Then the Pentagon Papers came out at about the same time and revealed that "the whole war was a lie from the start and showed the secret arrangements that were made between [Ngo Dinh] Diem and the Americans, that the Gulf of Tonkin attack on American ships was made up, and that body counts were wrong."

Radicals knew all of this, but the general public had been brought up on the propaganda of the fifties and sixties. Before that there was no popular support. "After Kent State, the Pentagon Papers, and then Cambodia, it became clear that the country was morally bankrupt," Michael says now, perhaps recalling the vicious physical and verbal attacks that antiwar demonstrators were subjected to in the early days of the Vietnam conflict.

Michael and Kau'i had been living together for a year before he moved up to Canada. She remained in California to finish her studies at Berkeley, and Michael, in spite of the obvious dangers, drove down at regular intervals to visit her. He had perfected a simple routine for his border crossings. Back then Seattle had a National League baseball team. Michael would arrive at the border a few hours before game time, sporting a team cap and saying how excited he was about going to the big game in Seattle. Then he would drive nonstop to California. And, just in case something went wrong, he carried alternate identification.

In May 1969 Kau'i decided to join Michael in Canada. She made a trip home to explain things to her Hawaiian family and met gentle resistance. "I knew they weren't particular supporters of this antiwar stuff," she says. "My father had wanted my brother to get involved in the war, but he hadn't gotten drafted because he forgot to register. Three of my older cousins were brought in by my dad to talk to me about going to Canada with a peacenik. One was army, one air force, and one was navy. That was the time when I told them what I thought about all this stuff, and my family thought it was quite disrespectful on my part. Within two days I left Hawaii in a huff."

When Kau'i first tried to come to Canada, the rules had changed and a six-month waiting period was required. The couple then travelled to Reno to get married before returning to the Canadian border, where Michael, who was a landed immigrant, was allowed to sponsor his spouse into the country. Kau'i became a landed immigrant an hour later. The couple settled in a house on the side of Burnaby Mountain and continued their schooling and political involvement. In 1970 Michael was elected vice president of the Simon Fraser University student society and eventually chairperson of the National Association of University Students. Kau'i was still active with the black student organization in Seattle. They once had a whole busload of students from this organization come and stay at their house.

In 1974 Kau'i began teaching at the Mount Currie Indian Band's community school, while Michael took a professional development year at SFU to qualify as a teacher. In 1976 he joined Kau'i at Mount Currie as a teacher. Kau'i became principal and Michael became Mr. Kau'i to the community. They stayed another four years, and Kau'i rediscovered her aboriginal roots, which led to her pointed comments about white men planning Indian conferences at the University of British Columbia. "It was a good time," recalls Michael. "It forced us to refocus our social and political commitments to daily life."

Michael has become a master at dealing with borders over the years. In 1994 he was travelling back to Canada from Southampton, England, where he was working on his doctorate. At a stopover in New York he was detained by the customs officers when his name came up on their computer. "They sent me off to this little room and asked me if I knew why my name had popped up on their list," Michael recalls. He spent two and a half hours in that room until he finally told the officers the truth – that he had come to Canada in 1968 to avoid the draft.

That was what the officers expected to hear, and they promptly let Michael go. Now Michael sees these little vexations as a sign that all is not forgotten in his parents' country. Still, none of this concerns either Michael or Kau'i very much. Today they are confirmed Canadians. Michael works with the Vancouver School Board and Simon Fraser University. He also serves on the board of a family foundation in the United States that funds environmental protection projects, including one in which a man travels around deserts and keeps an eye on the U.S. military, ensuring that they don't break any environmental laws.

Kau'i has continued her work with the First Nations of British Columbia. In 1995 she worked as a coordinator for the provincial government, dealing with issues around aboriginal education, and taught teachers' training for First Nations people at Simon Fraser University.

My personal contact with this remarkable couple has been slight but rewarding. I was one of those white men organizing the conference on First Nations education at UBC all those years ago when Kau'i remarked that "this looks like another conference being planned for Indian women by white men." At the time I took the young woman's hint and went on holidays. More recently I have worked with her on aboriginal education in the provincial government. When I reminded her of her comment 20 years earlier, she laughed and said, "Oh! That was in my radical days."

Radical, a word derived from the Latin *radicalis* – having roots – describes both Kau'i and Michael as well today as it did in the 1960s. Each has diverse roots that have fed bountiful and productive Canadian lives.

JIM BYRNES

Talking Vietnam Blues

"I always like to think of myself as Cacciato," says Jim Byrnes, referring to the title character in Tim O'Brien's novel *Going After Cacciato*. Written in a magic realist style, the book has Cacciato leave his company in war-ravaged Vietnam to strike out cross-country for France. Detailed to follow him and bring him back, his army buddies are led on a surrealistic chase across Asia and Europe. As fantastic as the fictional account is, Jim Byrnes speaks from personal experience when he says, "That's how it was."

Jim and I are having lunch in an Italian restaurant on Vancouver's Commercial Drive, and both of us are conscious of the thousands of miles and more than two decades that separate us from the Vietnam War. Jim has just returned from a trans-Canada tour marking the release of his new CD *That River* and is relaxing after a day of shooting *Highlander,* the television series in which he costars. Like many Vancouverites, I have been listening to Jim's music in downtown bars for more than a decade. A few weeks earlier I had watched him perform at the launch party for his new CD. On that occasion I had found myself reflecting on how long and hard Jim had worked to get to where he is now – a successful actor and a widely respected bluesman. In fact, in Vancouver he is *the* bluesman.

Jim's personal journey began in St. Louis, Missouri, in 1948, but his story in America actually started with his Irish ancestors who emigrated from Galway and went to work on the Missouri, Kansas & Texas Railroad a few decades earlier. Jim's father, the youngest son of a large family, was the first to be born in the United States and, in 1930, the first in the family to get a high school education. Toiling at everything from pipelining in Oklahoma to ushering at prize fights, Jim's father painstakingly worked to gain a degree and a college ring in 1944, which earned him an office job at the St. Louis city hall and a step up the ladder of the American Dream. However, it didn't give him a great deal more money, and the family remained essentially working-class. Other family members continued to work for the railway, more popularly known as the Katie Line, and as he grew older, Jim learned songs about it such as those by Yank Rochel and T-Bone Walker.

Also born to a large family, Jim's mother was a strong woman. Her father had died when she was only three and she had helped raise her nine siblings. In a time of large families, though, Jim only had two sisters. It was Jim's mother who brought music into the house, with her own singing and with piano lessons for each child upon turning five. When Jim was three, the family bought a house in the Baden neighbourhood of St. Louis. Named by earlier German settlers, the mostly Irish neighbourhood was making the transition to African-American during the fifties and sixties. "My parents went on living there until 1988, and my Uncle Joe and Aunt Dorothy stayed until the 1990s," says Jim. "They had been the first in our family to buy a house in America. It was the first place our family owned since Oliver Cromwell threw us out of our Irish homes 300 years before."

When he was very young, Jim had been deathly sick, and as a result, he had travelled twice a week for five years across town for eye treatments. It was on these bus trips that he saw how much poorer the black neighbourhoods were: "Pretty early on I realized there was this line that you crossed, but I didn't realize how bizarre racism was because it was all around," he says, recalling posters put up by the Reverend Billy J. Argas urging his white followers not "to put Negro music on your jukebox. Their screaming, savage beat and lyrics are undermining the morals of our white youth in America."

By the time he was 12, Jim had found all the great St. Louis AM stations, like KATZ, where he listened to deejays such as Spider Birks. But the music wasn't only on the radio. The blues had been coming up the Mississippi River from the Deep South and passing through St. Louis for a couple of hundred years, and more recently the soulful sounds of the northern industrial cities had been drifting back down. A lot of the music stayed in town. One of Jim's earliest musical memories is of African-American truck farmers coming down the street and singing their wares.

Now, as Jim and I drink our lattes in the restaurant, he sits back in his chair and gives me an idea of what he means, singing, "Strawberries, you get 'em three quarts for a dollar!" Grinning, he enthuses, "I was fascinated by the way they sounded. It was so cool. The blues were the older guys like Muddy Waters, Elmer James, and Howlin' Wolf. These guys had the direct connection with the country. Rhythm and blues were Ike and Tina Turner, The Orioles, and The Coasters. It was kind of a generational thing and more citified. But the blues were alive. When I got older, there were great blues bars that I discovered in St. Louis. After the cotton season in Mississippi, these guys would come through on their way north to Chicago for the winter. I also liked the Southern soul of guys like Otis Redding, James Carr, and Percy Sledge."

Like the river in the title of his latest album, the music flowed through the city and defined it. Chuck Berry had grown up in Jim's neighbourhood, and Berry's piano player, Johnnie Johnson, was a regular around town. Before he was old enough to get into bars legally, Jim hung out at the Imperial Lanes Bowling Alley. The Imperial's bar was adjacent and open to view from the bowling alley so that Jim could watch the house band, which featured Ike and Tina Turner, to his heart's content. "I didn't just learn the blues from records at college. I grew up with it in the air," he explains.

Jim was a good student and an earnest learner. In 1961 his solid marks won him entrance to a Jesuit high school where he became involved with drama, which led to private study with a professional theatre group. It was there that a California actor gave him a copy of "the book" – Jack Kerouac's *On the Road*. "That was a major experience in my life," Jim says. "To this day I still read it once a year. I love it. I fancied myself a bohemian. I had a perverse streak in me and I would seek out stuff that wasn't mainstream. Blues were accepted in the folk scene, and Sonny Terry and Brownie McGee would come to town and play the clubs. The drug thing was happening, and I was fascinated with that because drugs had always been considered a part of the blues and jazz worlds."

Kerouac gave Jim a path to follow. *On the Road* told him that he wasn't alone in his restless need to cross the musical and social boundaries of middle America. When he won a scholarship to Boston University in 1966 on the strength of both his academic and acting abilities, he felt as if he really were on the road. "I couldn't wait to get out of what I thought of as the cornball Midwest," he recalls. "I got to Boston and it was my first experience living away from home. By the second or third semester I realized I didn't have to go to school every day. I could smoke pot and chase girls. I put a band together with some guys in the dorm, and there was a whole big scene over in Cambridge at the Club 47. Junior Walker and all these blues guys would come there. I got into some left-wing political stuff and was very much into the antiwar movement."

These were the years when the strains of the cultural and political revolution played loud on the campuses of America. Jim made his own music and rode the sounds of the era. He dropped out of school, after a love affair went bad, and lost his educational deferment in 1967 while Country Joe McDonald, dripping sarcasm, sang, "Come on all of you big strong men, Uncle Sam needs your help again. He's got himself in a terrible jam way down yonder in Vietnam. So put down your books and pick up a gun. . . ."

It was also a dangerous time for a naive young Midwesterner from an Irish immigrant family: "I went for induction four times. I would get all drugged up and they would send me away and then I would get another letter in the mail telling me to report. I really didn't know what was right. I didn't want to let my folks down because they had always stood by me. I understood that either I stepped across the line and into the army or they would put me in jail. I had read that Che Guevera had said, 'The first responsibility of a revolutionary is to stay out of jail.' So I joined the U.S. Army."

The army sent Jim to Missouri for basic training and then out to California for light infantry school. "I kept thinking," he says, "that somewhere along the line the army would realize it had made a mistake and I didn't belong." But the army thought otherwise. After four months of training, he was mustered to Fort Lewis in Washington State and then flown out of Sea-Tac Airport to Vietnam, where he saw American racism laid out in a manner similar to the neighbourhoods of St. Louis: "The closer you got to the front, the more blacks you saw. I did a couple of assignments there," he offers without elaborating as we eat our salami sandwiches.

I ask for more details and he replies tersely, "After six months in action, I was back in Saigon. People there were really into drugs because they were readily available. I had gone over to Vietnam as a war protester, but once you're there, it's about you and your friends. It's us or them. No matter what you think about these guys, they're more like you than the other side is. It's about brotherhood. You never make friends like that again. You have a connection to those guys like you have to nobody else. Some of them made it back in one piece. Some of them never made it back at all. Some made it back in a thousand pieces."

It was these friends whom Jim worried about leaving behind when he decided to do as O'Brien's Cacciato does and get out of Vietnam, to go AWOL, to desert. As in O'Brien's novel, the only moral decision Jim faced involved leaving his buddies behind: "I spoke to a couple of friends and I just said, 'I can't do this anymore. The only way I'm going to survive this is to get out of here and I hope you don't hold this against me.' I talked my way onto an airplane and got back to San Francisco." When I ask Jim just how he "talked" his way onto an airplane, he smiles and says, "I was an actor, man."

In San Francisco he contacted some friends, threw away all his stuff, and went underground, doing a lot of drugs along the way. San Francisco in the late 1960s wasn't a friendly place for a Vietnam vet down on his luck, even if he had gone to the war as a protester and was now AWOL. "You realize that those who didn't go want to see you like they want another hole in their body, like they want a dose of the clap. You try to reach out and say, 'I'm on your side,' but no way. You weren't because you'd been there."

In *Going After Cacciato*, O'Brien's Vietnam wanderers ride through Yugoslavia in a VW van driven by a California girl who says: "The thing I can't get over . . . is that you dudes actually were *there*. I mean, like, you saw evil firsthand. Saw it and smelled it. The evil. Children getting toasted, the orphans, atrocities. And you had the guts to walk away. That's courage."

As in the novel, it was a time of absurdity, a time when people's minds were distorted by the experience of war as much as they might be by drugs. Reality was an illusion; survival was a dream.

Jim left San Francisco for St. Louis, where he hoped to find "a miracle. I really didn't know what I was doing, though. I was at a complete loss. When I got back home, I wanted to see my folks. I had spoken to them on the phone to tell them I was alive, that I was okay, but I couldn't tell them where I was. I felt so shitty. The FBI was already hanging around the house and harassing my folks. It was a really hard time for everybody."

Arranging to meet at a friend's place, Jim told his father, "I don't know what I'm going to do, but I've got to get out of here because I don't want to go to jail and I can't go back into the army. I think I've got to get out of the country."

"What are you going to do if you leave the country?" his father asked in shock. But then he gave Jim the names of some people in Toronto he knew through his union contacts.

"So I went to Toronto," Jim tells me. "I went across the border in October 1969. If they had turned me back, I would have jumped off the bridge. But oddly enough, when I got to the border, right ahead of me was this R & B group, the Detroit Emeralds, which had a big hit out called "Show Time." There were these eight black guys in green suits and the Canadian customs guys were just flipping. They saw me, this kid with a crew cut, and said, 'Yeah, go on through.'"

Jim looked up his contacts in Toronto and got a job sweeping floors at a record company, then applied for landed immigrant status. "I was hanging around Rochdale College [Toronto's "free" alternative school/co-op in the sixties and early seventies] and playing music. Then I got busted. This other guy and I were cruising the street when we got pulled over. He had some hash, but it was my car and I was driving. Next thing I knew I was in the Don Jail."

Jim didn't know many people, but the street community posted his bail, anyway. When he went to court, however, the judge wasn't quite so sympathetic. According to Jim, he said, "This man's an American citizen, and if he has no respect for his own laws, why would we expect him to respect the queen's laws? This man is the scum of the earth."

Jim found himself back in custody. A woman Jim knew had done some work for a well-known Toronto criminal lawyer and arranged for him to represent Jim. The man not only got Jim off on the drug charge, but he also got him landed immigrant status. "At this point I still wanted to play music, but I sure didn't want to be a drug addict. That whole scene down in Rochdale was getting weirder and weirder with the bikers taking over the drug trade and lots of bad drugs hitting the street."

Jim met a friend who had been to Tofino on the west coast of Vancouver Island. The friend praised the idyllic beauty of the place, and to Jim it sounded as if it might just be what he needed. He took a drive-away car to Edmonton and from there made his way to Vancouver. Eventually, in May 1971, he landed in Tofino and spent the summer in a squatter shack playing guitar around beach fires. Life there was good until the park officials evicted the squatters. Fall was fast approaching, anyway, so Jim moved to Sooke on the south coast of Vancouver Island. At the time Sooke was a noteworthy hippie community, and Jim soon found a shack that he was able to rent in exchange for looking after a woman's sheep.

"But I was frustrated," he recalls. "I really wanted to be an actor and musician. I broke up with a girl who went back to the States and I moved up the island to a friend's place at Errington. At this point I didn't know what I was going to do, but in February 1972 fate stepped in. A pickup truck had stalled on the highway and I was standing behind it when someone ran into it. I woke up in the hospital in Nanaimo. You need two signatures on a death certificate. One doctor was ready to sign, but the other said to wait a bit. Somehow I came to and told them how to contact my parents, then I lost consciousness again. A couple of days later I came to and the doctor told me I had lost both of my legs. My mother and younger sister had come up from the States expecting to bury me. I was so screwed up. The whole time from when I left to go into the army up to this point had been a complete fuck-up. My dad couldn't even make the trip because he was so busted up. I determined then that I would get back to the States, so I learned to walk again."

In due time Jim moved to Vancouver and started working as a musician, touring small towns in British Columbia and working hard to make it: "Nobody would believe I was an actor because I had lost my legs and had this big limp." Quietly Jim kept going to auditions but was usually turned down. On the music scene, though, he steadily built a following and eventually picked up some work doing voice-overs for commercials.

In 1974 he heard Richard Nixon's resignation speech on a car radio. Jim remembers being infuriated that the president could walk away from the mess he had created while people like himself were still considered felons by the U.S. government. "My commander-in-chief, as he had been once, was a lying son of a bitch," Jim says, the old anger welling up again. "I phoned my dad and told him to find me a lawyer because I was coming home. Then I went back to St. Louis and turned myself in at the place where I had been inducted. They didn't know what the hell to do with me. The fact that I had lost my legs confused things even more, so they sent me home."

Eventually Jim got a dishonourable discharge in the mail, which was later upgraded to a general discharge. Over the next few years he spent a lot of time travelling back and forth between Vancouver and cities like Chicago and Los Angeles, always looking for the break that would allow him to relax in the life that he loved. "In November 1977 I was working in a record store in Kansas City and I got up to go to work one day when I asked myself, 'Why?' So I got in my car and drove back to Vancouver and put a band together. I was an American citizen again, but all my friends were in Canada. I loved it up here."

He brought out his first album in 1981. Then, after acting in a few plays, he began to get a little movie work as Vancouver's reputation as Hollywood North blossomed. But the hard slogging of a musician's life continued, with stints as the opening act at the Commodore in Vancouver and regular gigs around the province.

Jim got an agent and continued to go to television and film auditions, usually only to be told, "That was really good. We'll phone you." Then, in 1987, the big break came: "I got a call to do a TV pilot for an American series, *Wise Guy*, for a role as a Vietnam vet cop in a wheelchair. On February 26, 1987, I was offered the contract. That was 15 years to the day since I had lost my legs. Since then a lot of good stuff has happened, both in acting and music."

The fact that he deserted from the U.S. Army remains with Jim as a central fact of who he is. He still won't tell me any war stories, though, and refers me once more to Tim O'Brien. Later, while reading *Going After Cacciato*, I find a telling comment made by an Iranian captain to an American lieutenant: "Without purpose men will run. They will act out their dreams, and they will run and run, like animals in a stampede. It is *purpose* that keeps men at their posts to fight. Only purpose." Like so many others, Jim Byrnes found no purpose in Vietnam.

These days *Highlander* keeps Jim Byrnes busy for a good part of the year. The series has allowed him to travel to great locales such as Scotland and, like Cacciato, France. He admits the work is demanding; when the show is shooting, he often spends 12 hours or more on the set. But the steady work lets him make the music that he loves without compromise; occasionally he even gets to play blues in the show. When he has a gig, he often goes directly from a day on the set to a night of singing.

Now, in the Italian restaurant on Commercial Drive, we have finished our lunch. The restaurant's sound system is playing an aria from an opera. I wonder what Jim is thinking about. Vietnam? His accident? Acting? Then he says, "I love this. I love all kinds of music. I like it when the guy singing sounds like he's gotta sing or blow up."

After Jim and I part company, I read one of O'Brien's short stories, "How to Write a True War Story," in which the narrator states, "And in the end, of course, a true war story is never about war. . . . It's about love and memory. It's about sorrow. It's about sisters who never write back and people who never listen." Jim has a purpose now, I realize, and people are listening.

FRED REED

Rebel with a Cause

FRED REED ANSWERS his telephone in French. When he patiently switches to English for someone who hasn't mastered his adoptive country's second official language, he maintains a slight Québécois accent. He gives the caller directions to his semidetached, red-brick house in Montreal's largely French-speaking area of Outremont. While he prepares coffee in his bright, modern kitchen, I take the opportunity to glance around the living room, with its tempting mix of books and research papers. On top of one stack of papers lies a publication entitled "Human Development Report, Albania 1995." On another pile sits a book, *Looking for the South: Contemplating Macedonian Poetry*. A number of other books bear titles in Greek orthography. Fred Reed, a tall, spare man dressed in light summer clothing, brings in a single cup of coffee, explaining that he doesn't drink it himself.

In response to my question about the Greek texts, he begins his story. Born in Los Angeles in June 1939, Fred is at least a good two years older than most of the people featured in this book. His mother came from a small town in California's great Central Valley. "I found out later," says Fred, "that somewhere in my mother's family tree there is some French-Canadian ancestry. Probably from Acadia, from the Great Dispersion [in the 18th century]."

Fred's father was born in Washington State to a mother who had emigrated from somewhere in the Austro-Hungarian Empire. He aspired to a career as an artist, but when his dreams were squelched by the death of his own father, he settled for a life working his way up through the ranks of the telephone company in Southern California. His mother, a graduate of Stanford University, was, according to Fred, "a woman of great talent, with a personality of iron." As a young man, Fred had a falling-out with his mother over her absolute insistence that he learn to play the piano. Fred won – and he lost. "I now seriously regret that I didn't learn to play," Fred reflects.

"Both of my parents were extremely conservative people in their personal habits, social lives, and political beliefs," he explains. Then he adds, "For reasons that I've never really been able to understand, early on in life I diverged from that kind of conservatism. I was considered an extremely rebellious youth. That's probably an understatement. In retrospect, I feel that, beginning in the early fifties, there were storm clouds forming on the far horizon and, somehow, I was affected by the impending tempest."

When he was about 15 years old, Fred started reading James Joyce, Dylan Thomas, and Karl Marx. At about the same time, a new family moved into Fred's cloistered neighbourhood. It was rumoured that the father of this new household had connections with the dreaded Communist Party. He had lost his job with a military contractor because he had refused to sign a loyalty oath, but he soon became Fred's mentor.

Given unlimited access to this man's library, Fred took happy advantage of it and began to encounter ideas that American society shunned in the fifties. "The literature wasn't subversive in an overtly political way. Rather, it was critical of the knowledge that we were belaboured with as young people growing up in the American school system. Questions were raised – if this is so, why not that? I became aware of social inequities. Why did blacks and Mexican people live in the crummy, run-down parts of town? Why couldn't they come over to our part of town?"

Nevertheless, schools were integrated, and Fred mixed with a good number of Spanish-speaking Chicano students there: "We were the islands in a sea of Spanish. The sea was lapping at our feet, but we wouldn't bend down to examine it." In spite of being discouraged from doing so, Fred maintained friendships with both black and Chicano kids at school. Most of his friends were athletes, but he also got to know some black kids from southern Mississippi, or "The Place," as it was known then.

Fred graduated from high school in 1957 and, following in his mother's footsteps, went to Stanford University. "I studied Russian language and literature, which reflected my growing interest in Marxism and its practical application in the Soviet Union. I found zero sympathy for my interests among my fellow students. Those were the most miserable years of my life. As time went on, I became more and more aware that this was not what I wanted to do. However, what it was that I should be doing was by no means clear to me."

But even at conservative Stanford University there were people with whom a young man, "who had more of a sense of what he wasn't than what he was," could connect. For example, there was an English teaching assistant who responded positively to some of Fred's writing. He did well in those courses that he liked and actually set out to fail those that he disliked – like the compulsory biology lab course, in which he succeeded in getting the lowest grade in the class. After two years of such triumphs, he left Stanford.

Fred headed for the University of California at Los Angeles next, where he entered the school of cinematography. This was more like it. He did some experimental work with a friend who later worked as a script consultant on Francis Ford Coppola's *Apocalypse Now*. It was with this same friend that he began frequenting the excellent bookstores that lined Hollywood Boulevard in those days. "One day I picked up a book called *Greek Passion* by an author who was totally unknown to me. His name was Nikos Kazantzakis. It was a book that turned my life upside down. In the space of two weeks I was so taken in by the world that it thrust in front of my eyes that I decided to abandon everything that I was doing and leave for Greece."

He enrolled in a two-month Greek language course and, in June 1960, left for Athens. He didn't know at the time, but he would not be returning to the United States. Although Vietnam was a topic of growing interest in the news, it would be some years before the pressure of the draft was really felt. And yet, at the same time, the draft had a very real presence for young Americans in 1960. "I was a child of the semiprosperous middle class, which meant that there was always some way of getting out of doing what you didn't want to do. Accordingly I got a deferment by concealing my trip abroad as further study. The insidious campaign to prepare the American public for broader involvement in Vietnam had already begun. Cuba would have been a pretext for an apocalyptic war with the Soviet Union, but Vietnam was the extension of the American empire or, in keeping with the domino theory, it was the government's attempt to stop the onrush of godless communism."

In Greece Fred discovered a new world, one in which people thought and acted differently than even an inquisitive young American product of the fifties could have conceived. It was a time when many young Greeks were openly contemptuous of American imperialism. "It was a big shock for me," Fred recalls, "but it was immensely cathartic and therapeutic. You could say that I went looking for trouble, and what self-respecting youth doesn't seek trouble in one way or another?"

He enrolled briefly in school in Greece, but then realized he was more interested in experiencing life than studying it. Fred soon learned that life there was tough, but he found ways of living very cheaply in Athens. "It was a beautiful city then, not the polluted monster we know today. The skies were clear and the nights were fragrant. The winters were barely cold and the summers were oppressively hot. It was gorgeous."

He explored Greece by tracing the footsteps of Kazantzakis, who had died a few years before. Cutting himself off from everything at home, Fred was, at times, miserably lonely. But he kept away from the expatriate American community. "I made it a point of honour to speak Greek, even my halting, broken Greek, everywhere I went. I had a little dictionary that I carried with me and the people responded to it. They would say, 'Ah, you're learning our language. God bless you.' They had infinite patience then, and took it as a compliment that someone wanted to learn their language. After two years I was speaking Greek almost fluently. After three years I had only a slight accent. It was then that I kept the pledge that I had made to myself back in California to try to translate one of Kazantzakis's works. I did, and it was published by Simon and Schuster in 1965. It was a previously untranslated travel book called *Journeys to the Morea*."

While Fred was studying Greek language and literature, he was also keeping himself informed of events at home. Because the United States was perceived as a powerful, and intrusive, empire, Fred was often challenged by the young Greek intellectuals with whom he associated: "They were aggressively critical of Americans. At first I reacted strongly. I had a sort of defensive mechanism, in spite of the fact that I didn't like the United States. Somehow I was still attached to it."

The first, and last, time that Fred voted in an American election was in November 1960 when he cast an absentee ballot for John F. Kennedy. But, disappointed, he came to see that American involvement in Vietnam was increasing, and felt that Kennedy wasn't doing enough to lessen the problems there. By the time of JFK's death in 1963, he had increased to 15,000 the number of American military advisers in South Vietnam, which had received $500 million in aid during that year. "It's too facile for me to say that I didn't believe in Kennedy, but I didn't think he was everything he pretended to be. My break with the United States had become complete. I realized there was a quickening of activity in Vietnam, and I started to get anxious about my draft deferral."

Fred managed to get his deferral extended for another year. Then he met the "tall, blond, statuesque Canadian woman of Nordic descent" who would later become, and still is, his wife. She was travelling around the world and had stopped in Athens when they met. In 1962 Fred told Ingeborg about his concerns regarding the draft. His parents were beginning to put pressure on him, insisting that he return to the United States and serve his country. While on a European trip, they came to Greece to bring Fred back home. "It started with dinner, then some cards were put on the table, and by the end of the evening the table had been overturned. They offered me money to go back and serve my two years. That was the ultimate blow. I said, 'You're trying to purchase my conscience. Go away!' I walked out on them. By then I didn't want the war, and I didn't want my country. All of it looks pretty simple in retrospect but, in the tenor of the times, it was difficult."

With the support of a strong circle of Greek friends and Ingeborg, Fred was able to resist his parents' pressure to return to the United States. However, in the winter of 1963 his second deferment ran out and he was notified to report in January for induction at an American army base in a suburb of Athens. "With my girlfriend and some other friends, we had a ceremonial bonfire on New Year's Eve of that year, in which I burnt all of my belongings, except my passport. The Rubicon had been crossed and the boats burnt on the shore. There was no going back."

Wondering where to go next, he considered the Scandinavian countries, the United Kingdom, Yugoslavia, and even Malta. Then Ingeborg suggested Canada. The couple contemplated marrying in order to make entry into Canada easier, but they weren't able to – at the time, civil ceremonies weren't permitted in Greece and, because of their personal beliefs, they wouldn't undergo a religious one. As it turned out, marriage wasn't necessary for Fred to gain landed immigrant status; he qualified on his own. In the spring of 1963 Ingeborg left for her home in Toronto, and Fred followed a month later by way of Halifax. "I knew even less about Canada than I did about Greece before I went there," he recalls. "There is no ignorance like American ignorance of Canada."

His entrance into Canada, however, was not without some difficulty. When he came off the ship in Halifax, Canadian immigration officers felt that a trunkful of books was inadequate capital to start a new life. It took a telegram to Ingeborg in Toronto, and her sponsorship, to get him released in order to proceed by train to meet his lover and her family. Fred enrolled in Greek studies at the University of Toronto but, upon hearing about a modern Greek studies program at McGill University, the couple, who had just celebrated their Canadian marriage, moved to Montreal where Ingeborg got work as a pharmacist. During his first few years in Canada, Fred and his new in-laws in Toronto were visited by the RCMP. His parents were also visited by the FBI in California. As one of the first draft evaders of the Vietnam era, it seems likely that Fred and his family were subjected to more intense scrutiny than the many thousands who would follow over the next decade.

Fred spent two years at McGill working on an academic career. But by 1967, when the couple's daughter was born, Fred had become "a full-fledged political radical." The war in Vietnam had escalated to monstrous proportions and "Life, as it is wont to, swept me off in another direction," he recounts. "As the war picked up, I became more and more involved in the antiwar movement. Early on I came to the conclusion that it was not only necessary to oppose the war, but to oppose the sociopolitical system that allowed such a war to take place.

The left was divided into these little chapels and we spent as much time disagreeing with each other as we did fighting the bourgeoisie."

The factions and subfactions within the antiwar movement existed in opposition to the right-wing warmongers, but ranged from centre to far left. Asked where he fitted into this spectrum, Fred answers without hesitation, "Very far to the left, extremely far. I was part of a group that started out as the Committee to Support the National Liberation Front of Vietnam, which did, of course, exactly what its name suggested, and upheld the view that it was necessary to oppose the American government's intervention in Vietnam."

It was also at this time that Fred published his first translation and began doing radio and film work for the Canadian Broadcasting Corporation and the National Film Board. Then, with his growing political involvement making it necessary for him to take up a more proletarian approach to his activism, he went to work in a garment factory as a cutter for 15 years. "It was a right of passage, but a painfully long one that I look back on with a certain wry amusement," he now says. Then he asks, "Am I prepared to weep about 15 wasted years? No!"

Over time the Committee to Support the National Liberation Front of Vietnam evolved and became the Canadian Party of Labour. "Somehow the focus on the war in Vietnam lessened and we began to turn more and more to social issues within a Canadian context, not the least of which was the Quebec National Movement," he says.

Fred's interest in the separatist movement in Quebec was emerging as a much more vibrant and better organized vehicle for the expression of his discontent than was the antiwar movement. He hadn't felt that he needed to learn French right away to live in Quebec: "It took me a couple of years to learn that there is a country here that has its own national characteristics and in which a majority language is spoken that I didn't know. So I couldn't live and communicate satisfactorily unless I did something about it."

Although he had learned the Greek language with relative ease, it took him until the mid-seventies to gain the fluency in French with which he now answers his telephone. Asked about the near victory of the separatist side in the 1995 referendum and the possibility of the political separation of Quebec from the rest of Canada, Fred draws on his life experience as a critic of the system: "It may sound callous and uncaring, but I say let there be turmoil. I'm extremely suspicious of doomsayers and naysayers, especially when they are backers of major industrialists. If it's going to discomfort them, then I say let's do it. I appreciate that this is a slightly idiosyncratic position, but I adopt it for a lot of reasons. I like swimming against the current. The strongest unions are those that are entered into voluntarily. The Canadian union is not a voluntary union and the so-called separatist approach is one of renegotiating the terms of union between two political equals. But speaking on a level of principle, and in terms of theory, I'm suspicious of nationalism."

All this talk of nationalism and the politics that surround and attempt to define it is both intensely personal and immediate as we sit in Fred's living room in Outremont. Since he abandoned his job in the factory in the late seventies, Fred has been working as a journalist and a translator. He has translated seven novels from Greek to English and has won a Governor General's Award for his translation from the French of *Imagining the Middle East.* In the past decade he has made numerous trips to Iran, reporting on events there in *Le Devoir* and *La Presse,* as well as on English-language CBC Radio and French-language Radio-Canada. In 1994 he published *Persian Postcards* with Vancouver's Talon Books, which explores some of the contemporary misconceptions and oversimplifications surrounding the modern Islamic state of Iran. When I visited him in the summer of 1995, he was looking forward to the publication of *Salonica Terminus,* also with Talon Books, in the spring of 1996.

In his introduction to *Persian Postcards,* Fred writes:

> As a journalist, I had acquired some understanding of the
> malleability of human consciousness that allowed practition-
> ers of our trade to be swept along by prevailing political

winds, or to be seduced – as the rabbit by the python – by *raison d'Etat*. As a former employee of a Canadian press conglomerate, I had gained insight into the way news is structured: not in the service of truth, but in the cause of increased revenue and its attendant sociopolitical considerations, or vice versa. As an ex-American, I had developed particular sensitivity to the dedication of the United States government to the promotion and protection of its imperial project, however fulsome the vocabulary in which the project is framed.

Common sense kept whispering in my ear. If the ruling establishment in the West so loathed Iran's new rulers, might these mysterious men of the cloth have a positive aspect?

Fred Reed's life, from those early days looking for intellectual space in California, through the student days in Athens, to the factory years in Canada and, most recently, the years of careful and methodical journalism, has rewarded him with the ability to observe and comment on such large political landscapes. If Quebec should separate from Canada, it would do well to keep Fred in the fold. His questions may not always be easy but, thus far, he has helped us all in our search for some answers.

RUTH ANDERSON

Journey out of Darkness

"WITH SHELLS THAT I gathered on the beach I made anklets. I wore them and walked across the camp and they set a rhythm that made me dance. I had never been musical, but now the earth remembered other drummers who had been on that beach. The earth taught me to dance."

Ruth Anderson explains this wonderful phenomenon as she sits at the dining room table of the minister's residence in a Vancouver suburb. It is her house. She is the minister. The time when the earth taught her to dance is a quarter century past, but she tells it with the immediacy of a cherished and oft-relived moment. It is one of many such bright moments that mark the path that brought her from a 1950s childhood in Virginia to this Canadian home. It has been a long journey, and the bright moments have been important beacons between some long and difficult stretches on the trail.

The journey that has taken Ruth so far through linear space and time has in other ways been circular. Her father was the Episcopalian minister in a small Virginia town when Ruth was born in 1945. "He was the newly ordained handsome young minister who came to the small town and married the prettiest girl in town. We lived in a wooden house on Court Street that looked ordinary then but was more like a mansion. There were two classes and we were in the 'good' class. The others were either black or poor white trash."

When Ruth was six, the family moved to a similar posting in another little Virginian town about 20 miles from Lynchburg, home of such Southern institutions as the John Birch Society and Jerry Falwell. She had already started to learn the rules of the legally enforced segregation of the era that applied to everything from bathrooms to churches. The Episcopalians had two churches in the town, one for blacks and the other, of which Ruth's father was in charge, for whites. "The only black person in our church was Wyatt, who had one arm and picked up the books after church. The best part of church was helping Wyatt pick up the books, but I'm sure I was very patronizing. I think I was curious all through my growing-up years about the black culture because it was forbidden and colourful and warm."

In 1954 the U.S. Supreme Court ruled that segregation was illegal, and Ruth recalls long discussions on the subject in her grade 4 class the following year. The children were asked what they would do if a "coloured" person was to come and sit beside them in the classroom. The white kids learned that the correct answer was "I would get up and leave."

The hope that the South would rise again was still alive in the Virginia school system. Ruth recalls: "We studied Virginia history for three years, all the presidents that had been born there. We studied Robert E. Lee not Ulysses S. Grant, not even Lincoln much.

Segregation was taught with the phrase 'separate but equal,' but we knew our old textbooks got packaged up and sent over to the coloured school."

Questions asked at home didn't get many answers. "How my father voted or how much money he made were things we weren't supposed to know anything about," she says, "so I was pretty foggy about what was right or wrong in that sphere, although we talked all the time about right or wrong in terms of religion. 'Love your neighbour, care for the poor, be with the oppressed' were major themes of Christianity that couldn't have been avoided, even in the South."

Ruth has intense memories about a young woman named Geraldine who was hired as a maid by her family. They had to build a separate toilet for her on the back porch, and Ruth's mother complained about "having to teach her everything," although Ruth recalls her as being a very wise woman. "I was growing into puberty with a young black woman who was beautiful to me, but my whole culture was saying that she was less than human and had babies out of wedlock and was poor. Of course, we only paid her $10 a month," Ruth recalls wryly.

Ruth describes her family in the days of those small Virginian towns as being "pre-middle class." Eventually, when they moved to suburban Louisville, Kentucky, in 1957, that era came to an end, and with it the gracious world her mother had known. Now they entered the American middle class in status but didn't have as much money as many of their neighbours. Ruth's mother was stranded among unfriendly strangers who remained so for the five years that the family lived in Kentucky. The schools were integrated, although the church was still entirely white. There was a period of culture shock for Ruth as she learned to be a teenager in the suburbs at the same time as she saw her mother suffer the damage that patriarchal America inflicts on a homebound woman. Ruth enjoyed the competition of the classroom but found the social competition more challenging. In time she worked out the new culture's rules, but in her senior year her father accepted a senior position with Bishop Pike of San Francisco. The family moved to Marin County, California, when Ruth was just three months short of her high school graduation.

Once again she had to learn a new set of social rules. But now that she was free of the rigid class strictures of the Old South, Ruth found her new life in California good. She graduated from high school and was accepted into Mills College for women on a full scholarship. While there she studied philosophy, religion, and sociology and excelled. Her classes included a good dose of what would today be called women's studies.

Located in Oakland, the college was surrounded by a thick row of eucalyptus trees. Within the campus, Spanish-style buildings were set out on beautiful grounds graced with polite young women and excellent academic instructors. "Outside the row of trees was an urban ghetto," says Ruth. "All the time I was inside the eucalyptus ivory tower being challenged and inspired, I was also drawn to get out of the tower and into reality. I used to take my books to a corner café and study there just to feel that I was a part of things. There was something in me that was rejecting the separation."

She graduated in 1967. By that time she had been involved in the Berkeley Free Speech Movement and had been in touch with the Civil Rights Movement. From there she had become involved in the Delano grape pickers' strike. After her second year of college, she had considered joining the Peace Corps but was discouraged by an adviser who had told her it would jeopardize her scholarship. This period was very influential in the development of her thinking. However, she says, "I was protected in my dormitory by the headmistress who came to the door in her nightgown if you were late."

With graduation the structure that had challenged her was removed. As a member of the Phi Beta Kappa academic society, she attended a graduation dinner where she was awarded a pin. When asked what she would do with her pin, she said she would put it on a bead necklace and go across the Bay to Haight-Ashbury and join the

Diggers. This was the Dutch-inspired group that worked to aid the growing number of flower children while exhorting everyone to tune in and drop out. But Ruth wasn't quite ready to drop out of the society that had nurtured her.

After working in a restaurant, she and her college boyfriend joined a couple of friends who were returning home to New York City. She spent a year there doing a job for which her only qualifications were her white skin and college degree. As a New York social worker, she went into the black ghetto of Bedford Stuyvesant, investigation notebook in hand, checking that single mothers receiving welfare were really poor. "The notebook was my protection. As long as I had it, I had power. We looked for television sets and men's shoes under the bed," she recalls with disgust. To grant any additional aid required permission from a supervisor on an upper floor of her office building. "I spent a lot of time crying in the elevator."

The experience confirmed Ruth's growing disillusionment with the system. She wanted to do social work, but not for New York City or anywhere "an expert had authority over dependents." At the same time she was becoming more attuned to the philosophy that said: "Simplify and live in glorified poverty." The people she knew were smoking pot and dropping acid as an integral part of this lifestyle. Ruth had her first experience with LSD with an older couple as guides. The husband, Roger, took her on a walk around Central Park and into a cathedral. "I remember in the cathedral," she says, "looking into a place of great fear and danger – the depth of the abyss – and having within me the courage to face that. It was an image that I have had my whole life. I know the darkness is there and I trust that I have within me what it takes to walk through. It was interesting that it happened in a cathedral, although I had left behind all sense of church and middle-class values at that time."

At the end of the walk they went to a little apartment where the wife, Marta, was making soup, and she showed Ruth how she kept all of the vegetable peelings to make stock. "I was impressed with her simple cooking. I had only seen people eat for their own satisfaction. Here the relationship between food and where it grows was honoured. She was teaching me something I hadn't been in touch with before. Roger talked and talked about what they had done in a commune somewhere in New Mexico."

Ruth knew then that the community Roger and Marta represented would someday be hers, too. In many ways it was the Christian dream of her childhood; it also had a connection to nature and the wholeness of creation. But she still held back from embracing all aspects of the counterculture. Shoplifting, panhandling, and free love conflicted too strongly with her life values. But, she says, "In the years of being a flower child I put everything that I knew on hold and was open to any new revelations of truth. I weighed them and came out not far from where I started. For a while I didn't say no to anything that others did. It was a real sad time of rejecting everything about my parents' lifestyle. Everything about the middle-class U.S. was wrong, which meant I also somewhat rejected my academic experience and certainly my connections to getting ahead and taking advantage of all the opportunities."

During her year in New York, Ruth's college boyfriend returned home to Berkeley. Some months later Ruth followed him. Back on the West Coast she finally left him because "I wanted to walk off into the sunset and he wanted to ride his motorcycle to work. He was interested in experimenting with the different fads that came along, but he wasn't prepared to leave the mainstream, and I was. I learned to honour and love the land, to honour my body, to look within myself for truth, to critique the society that we lived in, both Christianity and materialism. I didn't touch sexism until way later. In fact, in those hippie years I was a very oppressed woman."

At the beginning of the summer of 1968 Ruth hitchhiked with a girlfriend to the artists' community at Mendocino to visit a woman from her college days. They met a couple of men on the beach, strolled up a river with them, and stayed the night. For Ruth that night turned into a summer on the banks of the little river with Michael, one of the two men. "We did our laundry in the river and laid it out in the sun to dry. We cached our food in the trees, built a lean-to out of branches, and travelled to the mountains to camp."

Michael had been drafted and had done a tour of duty in Vietnam. Addicted to heroin, he had written a letter to the alternative press, chronicling the extent of drug involvement within the U.S. military, an action that earned him a dishonourable discharge. At the end of the summer he took a job on a commercial fishing boat and left Ruth and her bag of brown rice at a squatters' camp called the Meadow. "It looked magical to me," Ruth recalls. "Like little Hobbit houses made out of plastic and tarps. A couple of people had tree houses. We were very much a disrespected community by certain parts of society. Once we went into a church in Mendocino and one of the men got up in the pulpit and was preaching. Some women who were cleaning sat down and listened and then said that we were all children of God. So at that moment the church was embracing what we seemed to be about, but at the same time they sent the minister out to help a social worker take a child away from a young mother in the Meadow."

In the Meadow, Ruth made her home in a hollow tree. She loved her new life and her work in the communal kitchen. The Meadow was a place where the dream was working. Next door to her was a family that included a young man named Robert. One night he came to help Ruth check on a raccoon that was getting into her rice stash. When he suggested that he stay the night, Ruth heeded a book on Eastern religion that she had just read. It said that one who is wise and in touch with God would always be in touch with whatever life brings. So it seemed as if this were a spiritual message. Never say no if there is no reason to say no. "But I never fell in love with the man or particularly chose him," Ruth recalls. "It was just that he stayed the night and in the morning it seemed rude to ask him to leave. Robert told me not to use birth control because it put a woman out of cycle with the moon. Being in cycle with the moon was the most important thing to me after that. I thought I would get pregnant, but I didn't.

"It seems so shocking when I think of what I did," she continues. "But I do remember how it felt. It was exactly like it felt in Sunday school in Virginia and in Mills College as an A student. It felt like trying as hard as you can to learn the lessons that life gives and to find truth. What I loved most about the Meadow was waking up in the morning and lying on the ground, looking at the sky, dancing in the trees, swimming in the river, stirring a pot with sisters and brothers." But Ruth also found herself repeating her parents' patterns of male-dominated relations in her own relationship with Robert. "He told me that if I ever decided to leave to give him four days' notice. That was our contract. In the manner of that time he called me his 'old lady' and I called him my 'old man.'"

It was while staying with Robert that Ruth made one of her infrequent visits home. She now thinks she might have been subconsciously wishing that her mother would somehow force her away from the life she had embarked on. But, ironically, Ruth's mother was trying to accept, if not understand, her daughter's life choices. Ruth remembers with great fondness that, when it came time for her to hitchhike back to the Meadow, her parents bought her a set of long underwear and her mother drove out to the highway and dropped her off. Nothing was said during that short trip, but the kindness and acceptance of those acts remain an important memory for Ruth.

Robert had a degree in art from the University of North Carolina at Chapel Hill. He also had a drug problem. Ruth was fascinated by the intensity of his mood swings and how he stayed up all night reading Alice Bailey and other mystical writers. Even in her old man's striving to "get high," Ruth found a link with her Christian upbringing. "There was something in the addict pattern that was so intense," she says. "It was more important to get high than to eat well. That's true to Christianity. You're aiming for something more than life, and we had a good time in pursuit of something or other."

They bought a little Airstream trailer and were living in that when they received a traffic violation. Robert worried that he would be traced by a draft board that he had been asked to report to. The couple had recently met someone from Vancouver and now Robert said they should go there so he could escape the draft. Leaving the trailer, they hitchhiked to Seattle with their cat, a pile of books, and Robert's art folders. They got a ride to Vancouver with someone else and entered Canada riding in the back of a van as tourists on a day trip. Robert was certain he wouldn't be allowed into the country if his true identity was discovered by the customs officers.

Unable to find their contact in Vancouver, they followed the crowd in that summer of 1969 and headed across the Strait of Georgia to Long Beach on Vancouver Island's west coast. "It rained solid for the first week we were camped there, but then the sun came out and we moved down among the drift logs. As we lived on the beach and ate the local plants and slept on the ground, my roots shifted to here. I have felt ever since that I am an immigrant, but I belong on the B.C. coast. That was a good summer."

Ruth learned to bake clay beads in a can over the fire and sold them at a local shop. "The first time I earned enough to buy my own can of peanut butter I thought, I could live here." But Robert had other ideas, and in the fall they moved back to Vancouver. They lived for a time in an apartment on the edge of East Hastings, the city's skid row, and worked for a well-known hippie exploiter or entrepreneur who was refurbishing old brick buildings in what was becoming Gastown. When Robert's five-year-old child from an earlier marriage arrived, they moved out to a small farm in the Fraser Valley that doubled as a free school. The school folded, but they stayed for a time with an artist woman named Shirley, earning their keep by mucking out barns and tutoring the woman's three daughters. Shirley offered Ruth a way to live a marginal and self-sufficient lifestyle "without being so weird."

But Robert had difficulties with anyone Ruth got close to. Ruth was attracted to community, but Robert was antisocial. She hadn't used birth control since first being with Robert. Only now, on the idyllic farm, did she become pregnant. Finally, one day when Robert was at a bar in town with an ex-heroin addict, Ruth felt that since her baby would be born under the sign of Scorpio she needed to be near water. She hitchhiked to Galiano, one of the Gulf Islands, and liked what she saw so much that she went back to fetch Robert.

She brought him back in a camper van that belonged to a jewellery maker named Dan. They spent the summer hopping around the Gulf Islands, looking for a community to join. Then, late in the fall, they heard about a house at Shawnigan Lake on Vancouver Island where they might be welcome. They went to the house and moved in, but when the owner returned he explained that they couldn't stay on a long-term basis. Before they could find another place Ruth went into labour. She put a mattress on the kitchen table and, with the help of a midwife and "a whole group of people," gave birth to a boy after a 14-hour labour.

Still in hiding from the authorities, Robert couldn't do any work that required proper ID, so the little family continued to live on the fringes of society. Although they both had degrees, they did only menial labour. In the winter they moved from Shawnigan Lake to Sooke. The social isolation suited Robert and his paranoia grew. He maintained that if the authorities were to find him he would be deported to the United States, although there were many draft evaders around who had landed immigrant status.

In spite of this fear of the authorities they returned to the United States in the summer of 1971, taking their new baby to meet Ruth's family in the South. They lived briefly in the remains of an old stone house and then spent the winter in Ruth's grandmother's house, planning to buy farmland with Robert's brother. When spring came, the brothers' farm dreams evaporated. Ruth and Robert moved in with a woman who had inherited a plantation house in South Carolina. Once again Ruth found herself living in Southern opulence while poor blacks lived in the old slave quarters around the mansion.

However, life on the plantation proved to be a brief interlude before they moved on again to Pocatello, Idaho, where Robert had a distant relative. Their stay in Idaho lasted two years. Ruth worked in a day-care centre and Robert somehow managed to work in a factory. Then, just as Ruth began to feel settled in the community, Robert decided they should move back to Canada again. Ruth has never really known which of Robert's fears were real and which were fabricated to maintain control over her.

In Canada they rejoined their old friend Dan on Galiano Island. He had a partner named Francine and then another woman came to stay with them. Both of these women had had children on the same day. This little group moved to tiny Parker Island to join another couple and their three children. The community lived in teepees with a communal kitchen. Dan made musical instruments and there was good food and music, and life was idyllic on the little sandspit where they camped. Once again it seemed to Ruth that a community could form and survive. Dan was Jewish and offered an alternative to the Christianity that they all felt was compromised by its identification with the oppressors of contemporary North American life. The group decided to let Dan be their patriarch. He would tell them how things should be as they sat around the fire. But Robert soon grew uncomfortable and wanted his own fire. It was on that beach on Parker Island that the earth taught Ruth to dance through her shell anklets.

It was also to that beach that a little boat came one day bearing two men and a rifle. One of the newcomers, a draft dodger called the Hunter, shot a deer to help feed the little community. They tried to honour the animal as well as they could with their limited understanding of Native ways. The Hunter knew how to process the meat, which gave vitality to the people. And so the Hunter was welcomed and he stayed. But even as the people drew strength from the meat, their quasi make-believe world was crumbling. Robert wanted landed immigrant status and knew that if he married Ruth it would be easier, since she was already a landed immigrant. Ruth resisted the cynicism of an empty marriage but yielded, against her better judgement, to Robert's pressure. It was a tortured time for Ruth, one in which her childhood values clashed with the pragmatic moment. She no longer knew what the rules of life were. She recalls her time on Parker Island as "the place of worst confusion and disillusionment around the hippie dream."

The Hunter offered a way out and yet upheld the hope of an alternative lifestyle. His dark skin and quiet power represented a rejection of the racial tensions of Ruth's youth and the classist barriers of her college days. "I guess I was still stuck with my commitment to live differently," Ruth says. "I knew I wasn't living okay with my man. I didn't know any healthy route and I didn't at all critique my attraction to the Hunter. He was quiet. He looked like a Native man with his long black braid. He had deerskins, which he had tanned and which he slept in. He seemed wise and from another world." Then there was a night in July when she and the Hunter ran the little boat across the water. "The moon was full and we were going from our camp to another farm on Galiano for a harvest dance. It was like that scene where you ride off into the sunset with your handsome prince."

The ensuing triangle was devastating, and Ruth followed her prince to Vancouver. The Hunter had originally come from Chicago and had identity papers with a Japanese name. It was under that name that he and Ruth lived in the city. Somehow the Hunter managed to acquire a boat that had been padlocked to the dock for nonpayment of moorage. The Hunter could do things: he could fish and hunt and repair engines and make deals. Now he traded the boat to a couple who had a smaller boat but with a better engine. The Hunter and Ruth put a little woodstove on the boat and lived on board with Ruth's five-year-old son. Then they moved to another dock and began life on a larger boat. They were to fix the boat in return for living aboard it, but when they took the vessel over to visit Galiano

Island, the owner reported it stolen and the Hunter went to jail. Ruth continued to live on their little boat in False Creek, pumping the bilge and caring for her child between visits to the Hunter in the Oakalla jail.

She remembers during that whole period that she wanted desperately to "be right, to be not against the law," but by the time the Hunter was in jail, she also knew she had clearly left her middle-class upbringing well behind. Once, in the early days with the Hunter, she walked with him across the veranda of an old Vancouver house. "It looked a bit like a smaller version of my grandmother's house with a Southern-style porch. He was wearing pointed shoes and clothes from the Sally Ann. The way he was walking he looked like a person from a black ghetto. I watched myself walking out the door with him and thought, I have gone to the most forbidden place. It wasn't so much racial as going to the other side of the tracks."

But still Ruth adhered to the childhood family values that dictated you should do whatever you do well. "I had no other option but to prove that I was really, truly, supposed to be with him. I had totally succeeded in cutting myself off from the middle class. There was a hotel on Drake Street where I could sneak in the back door and get into the bathroom for a bath with my son, hoping that no one would notice. Other times we would bathe in the ladies' room at the Cecil Hotel on Granville Street."

When the Hunter got out of jail, he continued to live a strange life that was extremely hard on Ruth. When he did get any money, he would spend it on taxis and take friends out to dinner. Ruth would then have to borrow for the rest of the month. She now recognizes that she had been brought up in a patriarchal world that required a woman to live the life that her husband created. "He was a criminal and a woman can be a criminal's partner and there is a whole lot of law that is more sacred than the law of the land if you are a criminal or a drug addict. The same person who was trying to be good in school and graduated with honours was trying to walk a walk that she believed was hers. It was the hardest time I ever had. How does one be a good criminal's wife?"

They finally got their boat seaworthy enough to travel out of Vancouver to Gibsons on the Sunshine Coast. They lived on the wharf at Gibsons for the next couple of years. Ruth's son did correspondence schooling for grade 1 and a girl was born. The Hunter was still not a landed immigrant or a Canadian citizen, but somehow he managed to get a commercial fishing licence, using the assumed Japanese name.

Later they moved farther up the coast and settled in Sechelt Inlet. Two more boys were born, and life became even more difficult for Ruth. When the Hunter went away to fish, she lived the pastoral life of her dreams, but all too often his return brought violence. Finally a First Nations woman visited and extended the helping hand that gave her the strength both to leave the Hunter and begin a long and hazardous journey back to the society that she thought she had left behind at her California college.

She moved to another rural B.C. town and became involved in a church with a strongly charismatic minister, who was also a draft evader. The little church finally gave Ruth a place that was faithful to her dream of community. It was a homecoming in which her Christian values and sense of social responsibility were reawakened, and she discovered that she possessed a gift for leadership. Eventually, with the encouragement of the draft evader minister, Ruth enrolled in the seminary at the University of British Columbia and was ordained as a minister. She has her own parish in British Columbia's Lower Mainland, where she delivers sermons richly textured with the complexities of her life. Her talk is an inspiring blend of the best of the hippie dream with a more recent but equally heartfelt overlay of feminist values in a traditional setting.

For the people in the pews, most of whom have no idea about Ruth's journey, their minister's often difficult life experiences translate into her deep sense of caring. As I sit with Ruth in the dining room of her residence, she finishes her story and marvels at the rich complexity of her experiences and her emotions. She puzzles over the meaning of her quest for community and where it will take her in the future. She wonders about her own children growing up with a mother who has consistently rejected materialism in a society that has always celebrated possessions. It has been a long interview and the late spring sunlight falls across the hardwood floors of the dining room. Ruth takes one more look back into her past and says, "All I have left from that time is the moon. I still love the moon."

LESLIE GRAUER

Solitary Voyager

LESLIE GRAUER IS aboard his 28-foot mahogany-on-oak, Marconi-rigged sloop when I track him down. The sleek green hull sits gracefully anchored in the northwest arm of Halifax's harbour. A metal plate attached to the cabin door identifies the boat as a King's Cruiser, built in Göteborg, Sweden, in 1958. "The king of Sweden held a competition in 1950 to choose a design for an affordable family cruiser," Leslie explains. "When I saw that this boat was built in my maternal grandfather's hometown, I knew that I had to have it."

That was shortly after his move from Nelson, British Columbia, to Halifax in 1993. Leslie has moved around a good bit since he came to Canada to avoid being drafted into the Vietnam War in 1966. But he had grown tired of his parents', and America's, materialistic values some time before that. He understands the root of his parents' generation's elusive quest for material gratification and security, but he is aggressive in his determination not to be entrapped by it. His boat is, after all, not moored to the dock, but stands disdainfully just offshore, ready to raise sail and be gone at a moment's notice. A man of independent means with no need for a nine-to-five job, Leslie has attempted to create a harmony of place with his sailboat. It is a place, however, without roots; one that is constantly mobile.

Both of Leslie's parents were born to immigrant families in New York City. "Dad was born in 1911 and Mom in 1916," he says. "So my father was 18 when the stock market crashed in 1929, just when he was getting ready to go away to college. Mom was only 13 at the time, but she felt the effects of it nevertheless. Her father was a carpenter and a floor layer, and his business really suffered during the Depression. My dad was the oldest in a family of six kids and his father was a butcher."

In spite of the times, Leslie's father managed to go to college, graduate with a degree in business, and become a successful stockbroker on Wall Street. In many ways, then, he exemplified the success story of so many second-generation immigrants whose parents worked hard to provide their children with an education and a better life. But Leslie was unimpressed with the way in which his parents, and many of their contemporaries, lived their lives: "I would go to the country club with them and see all of these people who had more money than brains, and all they wanted to do was drink themselves silly. Somewhere in the back of my mind I realized that these weren't happy people. They had everything that money could buy, but they still weren't happy. They were nice enough people, but something told me that their priorities weren't what they should have been."

The idea of "quality time" had not yet entered the vocabulary of American parents in the fifties and early sixties, and Leslie understood that if he wanted to spend time with his father, it meant playing golf: "He played golf every chance he got," Leslie recalls. "I hardly knew the man. If I wanted to see him, I had to pick up the clubs. There I was, 12 or 13 years old, and every time I stood in front of the ball I'd get a golf lesson, 'Move this, change that,' so I didn't want to play anymore. I'd just as soon go off with some of my friends who were either members of the club or caddies. We'd go out and have a hell of a time. With my friends I learned that golf is actually a wonderful game. You could make it whatever you want. It could be extremely competitive, or you could just wander about in these nice fields and beat the ball around."

Needless to say, Leslie preferred the noncompetitive approach to golf then, and now, in a similar spirit, he prefers to sail his boat alone, purely for the enjoyment of the wind and sea. Just as he was urged by his father to master the sport of golf, he was also encouraged to excel in school: "I was told right from day one to take all of the academic courses so that I could go to college, get a good job, and wear a suit and tie."

By the time Leslie graduated from high school in 1963, he still wasn't committed to the idea of pursuing an academic education: "I wanted to design cars. Didn't every 17-year-old boy think he should design cars, just as every 17-year-old girl thought she should be an actress? I was going to study mechanical engineering, but I also applied to the Rhode Island School of Design, which was an art school. I thought that I might study architecture."

Leslie ended up going to art school and, after his first year, decided to study painting. Then he bought his first motorcycle. It was a little 175-cc model that he traded for a 500-cc bike, and then, finally, for a British Vincent 1,000-cc monster. "All this stuff had been beaten into my head to make me a good, honest citizen with a good job, where you had to wear a suit and tie. But I quit school after my second year. I was too busy riding my motorcycle. I didn't know what I wanted and I was just going to school to please my parents."

Leslie wasn't reading the rebellious literature of the late fifties and he didn't see *Rebel Without a Cause;* he didn't even know who James

Dean was. But he was experiencing the same kinds of things, in the same white American milieu, that these works explored. He had travelled a little – once with his parents to Bermuda at age 14, and then with his mother and a friend to look at colleges in the northeastern states when he was 16. He played some team sports with friends in the Long Island suburb to which his parents had moved when he was eight. He continued to participate in sports at school, but quit the track team when the coach kept getting after him for not working hard enough. He stayed with and enjoyed wrestling, though, in which he was able to set his own pace. But he recalls that once, "in one of the last tournaments, I was going to get an athletic letter just for having been on the team for four years. What you were really supposed to do was win one point in a big tournament. I was ranked seventh, but I thought that since I was going to get the letter, anyway, I should earn it. I ended up defeating a guy who was ranked second, and he was very upset about it. I don't blame him. He should have gone on to the rest of the tournament and won an athletic scholarship. He was a black guy from Port Jefferson. I feel bad about it now."

Leslie wasn't paying much attention to the civil rights or antiwar movements. In college he got into a crowd that was reading Bertrand Russell, who was writing about soldiers going off to war and shooting others who, in different circumstances, might be their friends. The ideas of Russell gave voice to Leslie's own sense of connection with others, like the Port Jefferson wrestler. In 1966, three years after graduating from high school, Leslie enrolled at Parsons School of Design in New York City. In his first year there, issues around the war in Vietnam were becoming more intense. The Gulf of Tonkin incident had escalated American involvement in Vietnam. By the end of 1965, American troops overseas had grown to number nearly 200,000 and the U.S. government was hungry for healthy young bodies. Upon graduating from high school, Leslie had reported to his draft board. At the time, it meant getting a draft card to use as identification for admission to New York bars. Now the card was taking on new significance. He had been notifying his draft board annually of his attendance at the Rhode Island School of Design, and then at Parsons, in order to maintain his student-deferment status. But now the draft board was demanding that students have at least a B average in order to maintain an academic exemption.

Leslie was living in a house in the Bronx with a few friends. Another student who lived in the house had a friend who was the editor of the *East Village Other*, an alternative newspaper. "We were sitting around in the spring of 1966 and I was worrying about the draft. This guy took me to meet his friend who handed me a copy of the paper with an article in it that said: 'Canada doesn't send back draft evaders. Problem solved!'" However, Leslie admits to being "like nearly all Americans at the time. I knew virtually nothing about Canada, except that it was north of our border."

There was a Dutch student at Parsons who had travelled in Canada and he informed Leslie that the best places to live were on the West Coast – either in Vancouver or Victoria. Leslie took him at his word. "I sold my motorcycle and a 1958 Porsche that I had bought earlier that summer. I got $600 and bought a v w van for $450. I was working at the golf course and my dad was paying my way through college, so I had a few dollars saved when I left."

Leslie left New York with about $500 in his pocket and drove west to cross the border at Niagara Falls. He was refused entry to Canada, however, because the border officials felt that he didn't have enough money to make it to Vancouver. Turning back into the United States, he proceeded on across the continent and entered Canada at Blaine, just south of Vancouver. "There was another fellow who came up with me," Leslie says. "He came to Vancouver and learned the printing trade. Then he went back to the States, joined the army, and printed up the notices that sent other people to Vietnam. He managed to get out of going there himself because he was in the government printing office sending everybody else over. What a cockeyed thing to do!"

After spending a few days in a cheap hotel in Vancouver, Leslie rented a room from Stephen Barrett, who was part-owner of the Bunkhouse Coffee Shop. Stephen got Leslie a job making beeswax candles and he began to meet people in the artists' community. In 1967 he followed the Expo 67 excitement all the way to Montreal with a girlfriend from Vancouver. His girlfriend got a job at McGill University's Redpath Museum, which put them in touch with Stanley Triggs, the curator of the Notman photo collection and an old acquaintance of Stephen Barrett's. With this newfound connection, Leslie got work in the library stacks of Sir George Williams University – known today as Concordia University. It was a closed-stack library and he was able to spend long hours indulging in his newly discovered joy of reading. "I studied comparative religions and philosophy while I waited for catalogue cards to be processed on the fifth floor."

After six months in Montreal, Leslie returned to Vancouver without his girlfriend. She was to follow once he got settled and landed a new job. When she didn't show up, Leslie went back to Montreal, only to discover that the relationship was over. "I just about gave it all up. I was so depressed, I said, 'Piss on it. I'm going to go back to the States and go to jail.' But Stanley Triggs told me not to be such a fool and managed to get me turned back around in the right direction. That was in November 1968."

At about the same time, Leslie got a notice from his draft board calling him to a preinduction physical on December 2, 1968. It stressed that there would be no appeal. "I walked into the American consulate and told them that I wanted to renounce my citizenship. 'Why do you want to do that?' they asked. I wasn't prepared to go to Vietnam under any circumstances and the only way I could see not going without breaking the law was to cease being a citizen of the United States. They asked me to write down my reasons for renouncing my citizenship, and somewhere I wrote that the land of the free and the home of the brave is just a fallacy. They got quite hostile,"

Leslie recalls without his usual smile. "They were very cold and wouldn't say anything that didn't need to be said. I was just some awful nuisance, like a sewer rat, that they had to deal with."

When he briefly took flying lessons in Vancouver, Leslie found a remarkable difference in the attitudes of people in the Canadian military. One of his instructors was an air force reservist who, on hearing Leslie's story, said, "Well, I would have felt obliged to go, but you are you and I am me. You have to live your life and I've got to live mine, so good luck to you."

"This was after I learned that two of my uncles refused to hear my name spoken and my father's best friend wanted to beat me up before I left," Leslie adds by way of contrast. He also recalls that his boss at the golf course, who had thought his work was good, wouldn't give him a letter of reference when he left for Canada. His father, though, was more supportive of his decision, insisting that he couldn't force his son to go to Vietnam because he wouldn't be able to live with himself if anything happened to him there.

On a number of other occasions Leslie was pleasantly surprised at the amount of support that he received from Canadians. "Just before I moved to Montreal Mom got a call from the FBI, which wanted the RCMP to question me. So I called the RCMP and went to see a sergeant whose brother-in-law was in the U.S. Air Force. He said, 'I can't understand this for the life of me. I agree with your decision 100 percent. My brother-in-law is going over there to fly these crazy missions and risk his life, and my sister is going to be a widow. It just doesn't make any sense.'"

Leslie sits back in the secure comfort of the cockpit of his beautiful sailboat and soaks in a little more of the August morning sun. He reflects on what he has been through and what it all means to him now, a quarter of a century later. "I realized then that Canada really is different from the United States, and it still is. In 1977, after Jimmy Carter's inauguration, I went down to live in Alabama for a while. I met a whole bunch of nice people, but I found that you couldn't have a realistic conversation with an American. America is always right. If you question them about their exploitation of Latin America, for example, they'll remind you of their foreign aid program and then contend that they're opposed to dictatorships. They still have the same hairs up their asses about Cuba. So nothing has changed."

There are millions of people in the United States who would vehemently disagree with Leslie, and many millions more around the world who would be hard-pressed to imagine someone renouncing his or her American citizenship. It may be that Leslie's rejection of his upbringing has inspired his fierce independence and rugged individualism. Reflecting on his life in Canada which, like most people's, has had its ups and downs with a lot of hard work along the way, he says, "I was always trying to conform to something nonconformist, but I could never quite pull it off. I was usually a little bit off to the side. I was never one for organizations. As soon as you get two or three people together, everything turns into a compromise. So if you have any principles, you have to give them up, because someone else is going to say that that isn't the way they want to do it. If I'm going to act on something, I might as well do it my way instead of someone else's."

And, clearly, Leslie Grauer has.

STEPHEN EATON HUME

Pugwash Patriot

STEPHEN HUME'S LIFE bears testament to the importance of grandparents in shaping the thinking of their descendants. Although they lived in dramatically different social and environmental settings, he recalls both his maternal and paternal grandparents with great fondness and respect. While his parents were trying to define a place for themselves in the highly prescriptive society of the fifties, it was left to Stephen's grandparents to provide the deeper values of family and community responsibilities. It is these values that one feels most strongly when visiting Stephen, his wife Karen, and their daughters Georgia, five, and Natalie, two, at their quiet suburban home in an older section of Victoria, British Columbia, where Stephen works in a provincial government communications office and writes children's books.

Stephen's political views reflect the strong influence of his multi-millionaire grandfather Cyrus Stephen Eaton, whom he visited regularly on his 3,000-acre summer estate at Upper Blandford, Nova Scotia. Like his other 13 Eaton cousins, Stephen spent a month of each summer of his childhood there, learning to love and respect the old man as well as the land that had bred him. Cyrus, not to be confused with Timothy of department-store fame, was born in Nova Scotia and moved to the United States as a young man to make his fortune as a financier. As a leader of the American capitalist elite, he eventually sat on the boards of companies that had interests in steel, oil, and railways. He was chairman of the board of the Chesapeake & Ohio Railway from the time he was 70 years old in 1954 until he was 90. But he had another, even more remarkable, side: at a time when most of his adopted country's leaders were threatening their opponents with nuclear destruction, Eaton was totally committed to finding ways for the nations of the world to live in harmony. He knew many of the world's Communist leaders personally and visited them often. In winter, when he wasn't travelling to the world's capitals as one of the proponents of East-West détente, he stayed at his 800-acre estate, 20 miles outside of Cleveland, Ohio.

Until he was about 12 years old, Stephen also spent part of his summer in the little Texas border town of Eagle Pass, where his paternal grandfather, David Hume, Sr., practised law. As a small-town lawyer, Hume took all cases and received payment in cash or kind. While he lived a comfortable middle-class life, he was a long remove from the eastern power-broker class of his son's in-laws. Stephen's time in Texas included rolling down desert highways at 100 miles per hour in his grandfather's big air-conditioned car from the fifties on the way to attend court cases in San Antonio, Houston, or El Paso. At that time there were still spittoons in the courtrooms for the lawyers' chewing tobacco. Stephen learned to appreciate his grandfather's lifestyle: they would go home together, enjoy a little Falstaff beer, and take a siesta. In the evenings he would hunt rabbits out of the back of a pickup truck with Sheriff Lyman. They would drive out across the desert with the shooters in the back and the rabbits bounding out of the headlights. The young Stephen's job was to go off into the darkness and kill the wounded rabbits. "They cried like humans," he recalls.

Stephen was born in Dallas, the second son of Cyrus Eaton's daughter, Farlee, in 1947. At the time, his father, a World War II submariner and lawyer, was still in the U.S. Navy. After following him to Hawaii where he was posted at Pearl Harbor in the early fifties, the family returned to the mainland to live on a farm just south of the Mason-Dixon line in rural Charles County, Maryland. It was an opulent life in a 1796 antebellum mansion on a farm that produced tobacco, corn, and soybeans. But it was a lonely life for a boy growing up with parents who were often not home and a father likely to be overbearing when he was. Stephen looked for warmth among the black families that lived and worked on the farm and in the house. Whenever his parents were away he would invite the black kids into the "big house."

A fine sweep of gravel drive encircled a big magnolia tree in front of the house, and it was here that Stephen was picked up most mornings in a Cadillac convertible driven by his father's bodyguard, Melvin. Stephen was driven to and picked up from the nearby Charlotte Hall Military Academy where he was a day student in the fifth and sixth grades. He has fond memories of Melvin picking him up with his girlfriend, who often had a copy of *Jet* magazine with her. The three of them would cruise the town in a car full of good talk and laughter. Stephen recalls, "Once Melvin told me that he was going to see James Brown at a place called Pope's Creek down on the lower Potomac River. I was so excited because I listened to James Brown on the black radio stations. When I saw Melvin again, he said that women had thrown their panties at James Brown, and I thought that was the most incredible thing."

Stephen believes that his father had trouble coping with the fact that he would always be overshadowed by his wildly successful father-in-law. His father had been raised in a "two-fisted" world where a man was expected to make his way through life as if he were John Wayne. He was also a Southern Democrat and carried a streak of his lawyer-father's humanitarian ways. When he ran for governor of the State of Maryland, he "went after the black vote" and was interviewed by representatives of the Afro-American press. As a result, he was decried as a "nigger lover" by his opponents and lost the campaign. His defeat left him a broken man and his behaviour became so outrageous that Stephen left home and spent his 15th summer hanging out in Ocean City. He got work as a lifeguard and continued to develop his increasingly independent nature.

By this time he was attending St. James, a tough Episcopalian boarding school modelled on Britain's public schools. He spent horrible winters at this dismal institution – from grades 8 to 12 – and graduated in 1965. Throughout these years he spent Christmases at home, stopped visiting his relatives in Texas, saw his parents through a divorce, and, in short, survived on his own. He not only survived, he did well in school and developed a fine sensitivity to the issues of the world and the shortcomings that surrounded him in his family and his nation.

The summers at Cyrus Eaton's Nova Scotia estate remain a high point of Stephen's childhood years. "When we were younger, we slept outside in tents, roughing it in the woods by the tennis courts. When we got older, we slept in the house, which was heated by fireplaces. Gramps had a butler and servants – the cook had been a chef on the C & O Railway – and at five in the morning I would be awakened by the sound of a servant coming into my cold bedroom and lighting the fireplace. Then I would have an hour of sleep listening to the pine logs snapping in the distance as the room heated up." It was an idyllic time and place, with boat trips to nearby islands for picnics where the *Wall Street Journal* was used to light campfire kindling. And always there was the presence of a larger-than-life grandfather.

In 1965, at 17 and with high school completed, Stephen enrolled in Trinity College, a small private Ivy League school in Hartford, Connecticut. He turned 18 in his first year there and registered for the draft as required. In the summer of 1966, after completing his freshman year of college and with American involvement in Vietnam increasing, he decided it was time to visit his grandfather Eaton.

Cyrus Eaton had garnered both widespread acclaim and condemnation for his friendships, not only with progressive Western thinkers such as Bertrand Russell, but with Communist leaders such as Nikita Khrushchev and Fidel Castro. In 1957 his sponsorship of the Pugwash Conferences at his Nova Scotia summer home brought together leading scientists from both sides of the iron curtain to explore avenues of peace. With the aid of a foundation established by Eaton for their continuation, the Pugwash Conferences are still held each year. In fact, the little town of Pugwash gained world fame when, in 1995, the Nobel Peace Prize was awarded jointly to the conferences and a founding member, Polish-born nuclear physicist Joseph Rotblat.

By 1966 Eaton, who had supported American involvement in World War II, was actively attempting to mediate de-escalation of the American presence in Vietnam. In a 1977 *New Yorker* profile he cites two of his military acquaintances on the Vietnam War: "Ike and Monty were the greatest soldiers of their time, and they both told me it was madness to send American troops to Vietnam and Cambodia, because we couldn't possibly win." In the same piece he also states: "Eisenhower explained to me in some detail that while North Vietnam was a small nation, it had as allies the Chinese, with the largest standing army on earth, and the Russians, with the most sophisticated military equipment. Montgomery told me that, to a military man, going into Vietnam was an absolute absurdity, and that anyone who was an army officer should resign rather than take part, because there was no chance of success. I suggested to Monty in June 1966, after we spent a day together at his country place in England, that he come over and talk President Johnson into getting out of Vietnam, but we were never able to work it out."

When young Stephen took the ferry to Yarmouth, Nova Scotia, and drove to his grandfather's estate that summer, he didn't know that Eaton had just been speaking to these two great generals. But he did know that Eaton was the one adult in his life whose opinion he could trust on his decision not to take part in the war in Vietnam.

"I drove to my grandfather's place and stayed two days. I was treated like a grown-up and would go to his bedroom every morning to talk. He was very formal, but very warm and very big. Not in a physical sense, but what a mind he had! I told him I opposed the war and wanted to go to Canada, and he offered his complete support. Not only did he support me, but he reinforced my decision to leave the United States and settle in Canada." Of equal importance, Eaton also encouraged his grandson's poetic aspirations at the time. "He took poetry seriously. It wasn't some dilettante, effete bullshit for him. I said that I wanted to be a poet and he entirely approved."

Over those two days Stephen and his grandfather discussed the virtual holocaust taking place in Vietnam. "The American government was committing genocide on the Vietnamese. The *New York Times* was reporting it. We were dropping napalm on villages, children were being killed and burned. No one understood why they were trying to win a war by destroying not just North Vietnam, but South Vietnam, as well. *Ramparts* magazine was reporting corruption. A few priests, rabbis, and ministers were against the war, and for me that was important. Religion was important to me then. Buddhist priests were burning themselves to death in front of the U.S. embassy in Saigon. An American Quaker immolated himself in protest against the war."

With the invaluable moral support of his grandfather, Stephen returned to Trinity College knowing that when the time came, he would go to Canada. Shortly after returning to the college he decided to participate in the October 1967 march on the Pentagon. The irony of his father having worked at a desk in that very building didn't escape him.

"I went down to that march with one of my teachers, a veteran of World War II. My mother was living in Washington at the time, but I went straight to the march. I was amazed at how many people there were. There were soldiers teargassing men and women. Some women were there with baby carriages because they didn't think it would be violent. It was ugly. Then there was a lull and one of the officers from a line of military police came forward and said, 'You people stay there. Anyone who moves forward will be arrested.'

"I walked straight up to him and I got down on my knees and put my hands behind my back. He said, 'Get up and go back.'

"A black military policeman came out of the line and grabbed me, whacked me on the head with a truncheon, and then pulled me along the ground as hard as he could so that the dirt went down the front of my shirt and into my pants. He kept hitting me as he dragged me along and then he jerked me up and put his face next to mine and asked, 'Are you okay?'

"It's as if he was saying, 'I'm doing my job, but I understand what you are doing and I care about you.'

"I said, 'Yeah, I'm okay.'

"He said, 'Stay here and someone will come and get you.'"

Stephen and other protesters were put in a bus with wire mesh on the windows and then driven to the state prison in Lorton, Virginia. There were several hundred people who spent the night there on army cots. The next morning, Stephen recounts, "There was a line-up for breakfast, and in front of me there was this little short white guy with kinky hair and a three-piece suit that was all wrinkled from being slept in. Turns out it was Norman Mailer! He looked at me and said the famous words, 'What are we having for breakfast?'"

After breakfast, in which the choice was cornflakes or white cake with icing, the protesters were taken before a judge, where Stephen promised, "even though I didn't mean it," never to go within 200 yards of the Pentagon again. When he got back to Trinity, he wrote an article about the incident for the student newspaper. When he submitted his piece, the editor said, "This is shit, Hume. We're going to have to write a counterpoint against you and these war protesters."

The counterpoint article was written and ran with Stephen's piece. "Most of the response I got was: 'You fucking traitor.'" Although he does recall that there were some who agreed with him. In fact, Stephen notes that within two or three years of the publication of his article, the majority view had changed to oppose the war. "Even my mother, who at the time of my arrest was in favour of the war, changed to oppose it."

The professor with whom Stephen had gone to the Pentagon demonstration became his draft adviser and explained his range of options, including declaring himself a conscientious objector, going to Sweden or Canada, going to jail, or doing alternative service as part of the CO status. "I told him I couldn't declare CO status because at that point I had no compunction against killing. In fact, at the time I was a hunter, had gone to a military academy, and was a member of the National Rifle Association. If it had been a different war, I might have enlisted, but I believed that doing so for this war would have made me no different than the 'good Germans' who fought for Hitler."

Stephen graduated from Trinity in the spring of 1969. Two days after graduation he piled all of his books into his Volkswagen and drove to Niagara Falls, New York. Following the directions of his adviser, he cut his hair and bought a suit and a briefcase in preparation for crossing the border. On the Canadian side of Niagara Falls he filled out the appropriate forms to apply for landed immigrant status, again just as his adviser had told him, and was admitted into Canada immediately.

He had already been accepted into graduate school at both the University of Chicago and the University of Toronto. He showed up at the latter, feeling pretty good about himself for having chosen

Canada as his new home. However, they weren't impressed at the university when he applied for housing: "They basically said, 'Who do you think you are, you chauvinistic American? We don't owe you anything. We don't even like Americans.'

"It wasn't their fault. It was my fault," he now realizes. "I think I arrived assuming that they were going to do something for me because I had resisted the war. Now that I look back on it, I think I would have done the same thing in their position."

Stephen completed his M.A. in English over the next two years and got a job with the Toronto Women's Collective counselling people on birth control and sexually transmitted diseases. After about a year on the job, he moved to Ottawa, became a Buddhist, and worked in a commercial greenhouse. Then two doctors diagnosed him with Hodgkin's disease. He was given three to six months to live. "I was angry. They wanted to operate on my thyroid to extend my life for a little while. I told them that I would rather die than go into the hospital."

Instead, he bought a book on yoga that taught self-healing through meditation and chanting. "I know it sounds funny, but I watched television once a week – the show with that guy, Kwai Chang Caine, the Chinese martial artist in the Wild West," Stephen says in reference to David Carradine in *Kung Fu*. "Every night I did these meditation exercises – chanting 'I am the sun. The sun is in me. The sun is burning out all of the impurities in me' – until sweat poured out of me. I took it very seriously because conquering this thing was all there was."

Within a few months of being diagnosed, Stephen moved to Victoria on Vancouver Island where he could live near mountains and water. He continued the meditation and landed a job at the Victoria *Times-Colonist* newspaper, eventually concentrating on investigative work. He had published some erotic poetry and been included in an anthology of young poets, but had no other credentials. "They had a cafeteria then, before Thomson Newspapers took it over. I had been a vegetarian, but the Indo-Canadian cook said I was too skinny and gave me meat. I began to gain weight. After about a year, I realized that I had a job, I wasn't dead, and everything was fine."

Stephen continues to live and write in Victoria. He has put down roots with his family and created a life that in many ways reflects the values of the grandparents who influenced him. At the same time, however, it is a life that he has made unique. He went to see his father before moving to Canada and found him in rough shape on the Maryland farm, still being cared for by Melvin. His father later returned to Texas, where he died in 1971. Stephen's mother lived in a private nursing home in Nova Scotia until her death in 1995. Her son scattered her ashes in the Strait of Juan de Fuca on a route taken by migrating pods of whales – it was her wish.

Cyrus Eaton died in 1979, but not before he had read and approved of much of Stephen's poetry. On April 25, 1975, the 91-year-old Eaton wrote to Stephen from his office in the Terminal Tower, Cleveland, Ohio, to congratulate him on becoming a Canadian citizen and to say, "I am also delighted to know that you have completed four more poems. You will make us all famous with your brilliant pen." His grandfather's letter goes on to say, "I am in daily touch with the leaders in Cambodia and North and South Vietnam and am working hard with our government officials to persuade them to terminate our unwise and unhappy involvement in Southeast Asia."

But Eaton wasn't always pleased with Stephen's poetry. "I wrote some poems that he wasn't happy with. They were erotic and he didn't really understand them. He liked my political poems, like the one on his friend Salvador Allende, the Chilean president who was killed by the CIA," Stephen recalls.

Issues around the war in Vietnam are still emotionally charged for Stephen. One of his favourite authors is Tim O'Brien, a Vietnam veteran. In one of O'Brien's short stories, "On the Rainy River," a young man, ostensibly O'Brien, plans to swim to Canada from a rowboat on a Minnesota river. He's only 30 yards off the Canadian shore, but in the end decides not to go. The young man says he isn't brave enough to leave and face the criticism of family and friends. He sees himself as a coward and goes off to the war.

Stephen's feelings about Vietnam were rekindled when former defence secretary Robert McNamara published his recollections of the war in 1995. Stephen tells of "the widow of Norman Morrison, the Quaker who burned himself to death outside McNamara's Pentagon office in 1965 to protest the war in Vietnam – she wrote a letter thanking McNamara for writing the book, which acknowledged that the war was wrong. I don't care how many black walls they build in Washington for Americans who died. They'll never build a wall big enough to carry the names of all the Vietnamese children who were killed or mutilated by napalm, and the families torn apart, and the kids who were born with defects from the defoliants sprayed by American planes, and the villages set on fire. Give me a Vietnam memorial for that! This was a high-tech war of extermination waged by corrupt politicians. I feel that there is still a lot of American narcissism about the war. Many people were slaughtered – 58,000 Americans and three million Vietnamese. My grandfather said, 'No one could win that war. It was insane.' He was right."

JOHN HAGAN

Country Joe in Academia

IT IS A BIG GREY sandstone house on a quiet, tree-lined street of
similar homes in a neighbourhood in Metropolitan Toronto's North
York. Built in 1927 by an earlier wave of immigrants who prospered
in their new country, it is now the home of another first-generation
Canadian, John Hagan. As with earlier waves of immigrants,
American-born Hagan has done as much for Canada as Canada has
done for him. He comes, after all, from that generation of Americans
who heeded John F. Kennedy's plea to "Ask not what your country
can do for you, but what you can do for your country."

But such fine ideals have their moral limits. When John's country
asked for his support in its undeclared war in Vietnam, he turned his
back on his homeland and devoted his life to service in Canada

instead. By the nineties John's academic career had taken him to the University of Toronto, where he still teaches courses and conducts research in both the faculties of sociology and law. This interesting mix of disciplines stems in part from his Ph.D. thesis, which he wrote at the University of Alberta in Edmonton. In his dissertation John examines the sociological reasons behind the wide disparity in the ratio of First Nations people in Canadian jails relative to their representation in the general population. John is quick to point out that his current position also has much to do with his rich and varied home life as a child.

John was born in 1946 in Urbana, where his father, a political scientist interested in the American government, taught at the University of Illinois. After raising the children, John's mother also undertook an academic career. She studied musicology and, not unlike John's father, was interested in the sociological aspects of the field. His parents raised him to be conscious of an American citizen's political responsibilities: "I guess you could say both of my parents were, to a certain extent, activists. My father ran for city council as a socialist when I was a child, and they were both involved in Norman Thomas's Socialist Party before I was born." In later years, however, having recognized how difficult it is to get elected on a socialist ticket in the United States, they became active in the Democratic Party.

John's parents also brought an interesting mix of cultural roots to the family. "My mother was a Russian-Polish Jew from New York and my father was an Irish Catholic from Tennessee, where his family had been lawyers and plantation owners. They regarded themselves, first and foremost, as liberal humanists." In spite of his rich cultural background, John's childhood didn't differ dramatically from other middle-class, middle-American kids growing up in the suburbs. Urbana was a pleasant college town, but even it had a black ghetto. The black community straddled the railway tracks that divided Urbana and Champaign, and drew people from the massive northward migration of Afro-Americans of the era. Black kids dominated the school sports teams, but they were seldom seen at the community recreation centre. "I don't think that friendships crossed race lines that much. They did a bit, but we went over into that neighbourhood mostly to eat at a restaurant called Poor Boys, where they served Polish sausages with hot barbecue sauce."

John graduated from Urbana High School in 1964 and then from the University of Illinois in 1968 with a degree in sociology. "The University of Illinois was the elite school in the state college system and there weren't a lot of black students there," John recalls. "But I can remember my father helping young black scholars to find housing and encouraging them to apply for graduate school. That was quite unusual at the time."

No one in John's high school graduating class was talking about Vietnam in 1964. However, just three years later, the silence was broken. John and his peers were required to take an exam to see if they could maintain their student deferments. "There was something about disqualifying some students on the basis of low marks. I don't know if they ever actually did anything with those marks," he says. Then he adds, with a note of wonder in his voice, "As soon as I say that they even had such a test, it sounds incredible. They actually thought that they could get away with that. But then how did they think they could run a draft in such a racially and class-biased way? At the same time, it must be recognized that when young, less-educated blacks were being drafted into a peacetime army it was seen as a means of upward mobility. When they started being killed by the thousands, the government began to examine deferments that were benefitting more whites."

The 1967-68 academic year saw a dramatic increase in anti-Vietnam student awareness on the Midwestern campuses of the United States. Many students, including John, hitchhiked to San Francisco that summer and experienced the counterculture of peace and love that was flourishing in Haight-Ashbury. The ideals of peaceful revolution, with the slogan "Make Love Not War," came flowing back across the Rocky Mountains and the cornfields to take root in the fertile flatlands. "In the spring of 1968 the draft became a major focus of life. I started to take notice of the tables set up in the student union building by antidraft groups. The Toronto Antidraft League was there and gave out a pamphlet that was very professionally done and full of useful information on how to immigrate to Canada and what the different cities were like."

By the time John completed his bachelor's degree, graduate school deferments were being eliminated, so he decided to take a teaching position in a poor black neighbourhood on Chicago's south side in order to maintain a teaching deferment. "About the middle of that year Jessie Jackson began running an operation called PUSH. One of the policies of that project was to get the white draft dodgers out of the black schools on the south side. They wanted black teachers for black students and I could see their point, so I left."

John next attempted to maintain a deferment by joining VISTA, a kind of stay-at-home, or domestic, Peace Corps. He had married while he was teaching, and now both he and his wife joined. After a training period, during which the couple lived with a black family, they were assigned to a small town in Oklahoma where the antipoverty program was run by the son of the local banker. "We went through what everyone goes through when you are assigned to a small town. You are trained in organizational work and then, ultimately, you become involved in organizing against the local poverty program when you discover it is merely an extension of the local power structure. In this case it was a political appointment by the Johnson administration and the local Democratic Party. It was perhaps the biggest source of external money in town," John recalls, smiling at his youthful naivety.

John and his wife learned and grew from their experience in Oklahoma and were then assigned to a new town, Marshall, in northeast Texas. "It was there that we started a community newspaper, dealing with local issues around education and inclusion of the black settlements on the edges of town in the public sewer services. The idea behind the Johnson administration and the more liberal inclinations of the Democratic Party was that if you just give a little more organization and cohesion you will create an atmosphere for social change."

Even the name of the town, Marshall, conjures up scary images of back roads and potbellied sheriffs in the mind of the average Canadian. The movie *Easy Rider* hadn't been made yet, but the decade's news was filled with one horror story after another about what happens to "troublemaking northerners" in small Southern towns. "Yes, we were very nervous, and we were convinced that we weren't just upsetting local people, but the FBI, as well. We'll never know for sure, but we thought our phone was tapped," John recalls. "In the second issue of the newspaper we published a cartoon of a statue in the town square. It commemorated the role of the Knights of the Golden Circle militia group in the Civil War. The cartoon depicted the statue reduced to a pile of rubble."

The ability of government to be the vehicle of its own reform through projects like VISTA was being questioned on many fronts, both liberal and conservative. John draws a parallel between the stated aims of the Vietnam Village Pacification Program and the war on poverty in the United States. He points out that in both cases American establishment values of community and economic development would be given to the poor in Vietnam or in the American South and they would welcome the opportunity to share in the "good life." With growing self-doubt, word of trouble brewing overseas, and acceptance letters to Canadian graduate schools arriving in the mail, John and his wife agreed that it was time to leave for Canada. They decided to move to Edmonton because John wanted to study both sociology and criminology, and these disciplines were strongly represented at the University of Alberta. "I was always interested in issues of class, race, and social behaviour, and crime is a big part of all of that."

In August 1969 John and his wife applied for landed immigrant status in exactly the manner that the Toronto Antidraft League pamphlet had prescribed. "When I told my father that I was going to Canada, he told me that it was the biggest mistake I could ever make. He felt that I should just go into the army and obtain a noncombatant role. He believed in America. He believed in being a force for change within American society, and that that provided the opportunity and prospect for things to become better. He thought that in leaving the United States I would not be making the contribution that I should make."

John's parents had always given him a tremendous amount of independence and his father presented his concerns without placing any pressure on him. But John didn't want to have anything to do "with the crazy phenomenon of killing people and the senseless loss of lives. I didn't want to participate in any way. I didn't even want to be in a country that was doing this."

So John and his wife crossed the border into Manitoba and drove westward along the Trans-Canada Highway to Edmonton. "At that time Canada was a bit behind the United States. There was no cable television with American stations in Edmonton, and no McDonald's restaurants. But the University of Alberta was a big school with a good library, and a friend of mine had also moved there the year before to avoid the draft."

Things went well for John during the five years that he lived in Alberta. He quickly got a position as a teaching assistant and, in 1971, he got a Canada Council Doctoral Fellowship. He recalls demonstrations against local contractors who were profiteering from sales to the American military. He participated in these, but he wasn't an organizer. It was while lecturing at the University of Alberta that the American government finally granted him an occupational deferment, the day before the Johnson administration eliminated them. By this time the deferment was of minimal interest to him, as his focus was now on his research documenting the inequities suffered by Native people in the criminal justice system. "But it was all so different than the American situation," John says of his study. "I had funding from the provincial government to do this work, and when I finished, I gave a report at the annual meeting of the Provincial Judges Association. I doubt that anything was ever changed, but at least they listened and acknowledged that there was an injustice. Compared to black people in the United States, the socioeconomic problems of Native people in Canada seemed to stem a lot more from alcohol-related crime."

In 1974, having completed his Ph.D., John began working out of the University of Toronto's Erindale College on a study of 800 high school students in the Toronto suburb of Mississauga. The study examined the students' experiences in school and at home as they related to involvement in delinquent behaviour. About 500 of these same students were interviewed for a follow-up project in 1989. John's research demonstrated that those students from more impoverished backgrounds were more likely to act delinquently than those from more affluent homes.

This study, with its potential for tracking patterns of behaviour over generations, is just a part of John's extensive work in Canada that has resulted in the publication of over 130 papers and nearly a dozen books. Each of his works contributes to our understanding of the Canadian political and justice systems as they affect ordinary citizens.

In 1975 John accepted a tenure-track position at the University of Toronto. He could have returned to the United States, but his life was now comfortably established in his new country. "I have since gone back and forth to the United States. I went to lecture at the University of Indiana in 1977 and at the University of Wisconsin in 1980. I think over the years, as I have become more Canadian, it becomes increasingly uncomfortable for me over there. I mentioned being a draft dodger to a class in Wisconsin once, but I don't think I'll bring it up when I go down there in the future. It is such an abstract idea for students today. I think their attitude is, 'Why are you telling us this?' I do always tell my students in Canada that I grew up in the United States, but that I've spent more time here than I have there. I do this, in part, to explain why I tend to talk more about American crime than other professors. I feel they need to know who they are listening and talking to. I don't think that my experience as a draft dodger means much to them either, but I guess I feel it is important that they know."

For many draft resisters who have remained in Canada, the uncertainty surrounding one's identity is a common experience. "One of the things that struck me most about being who I am in Canada," John muses, "came from a *Globe and Mail* film review by Jay Scott, who was himself a draft dodger. The film was a documentary about draft evaders in Canada, entitled *America: Love It or Leave It*. Scott noted that Americans are probably the only group in Canada who really aren't able to comfortably maintain and embrace their old national identity. I had always known this to be true, but I had never been able to articulate it."

While John's feelings undoubtedly have a great deal of validity, they are not entirely at odds with those of other first-generation immigrant groups, who often feel a need to suppress their cultural backgrounds in order to fully develop a Canadian identity. John's son, a second-generation, hockey-playing Canadian, is now reclaiming a piece of his ancestral heritage – on the wall of his bedroom hangs an American flag. I found this to be personally interesting, having been raised by an American-born mother who was highly distrustful of the American way. Yet I, too, find myself constantly compelled to try to better understand the true nature of society in the United States.

John's next project may give us all a deeper understanding of Americans in Canada, as he plans to deal with the very subject of this book – Vietnam-era draft evaders currently living in this country – in a comprehensive academic study. The study will take a number of years, and John hopes that his profile in this book may encourage others like himself to contact him at the University of Toronto.

The kitchen and dining room of John's house glow with warm light reflected off well-finished oak. Sitting on the sideboard by the telephone is an old classic – a mid-sixties Country Joe McDonald album, *I-Feel-Like-I'm-Fixin'-to-Die*, with the irreverent Fish Cheer. "We had a garage sale last week and sold all of our old vinyl records, but I pulled that one out of the pile," explains John. There are some important cultural artifacts that even the most ardent immigrant can't discard.

PAUL GEORGE

Showman of the Rainforest

"A CATHEDRAL FOREST is a far better spectacle than any light show we ever had," says ex-rock band promoter turned environmentalist Paul George. As he speaks, a vision of soft light streaming through a forest canopy to dapple the ground dances in his eyes. Paul is a storyteller working in images. He learned the joy of fluid colour in the light shows he once produced for 1960s psychedelic rock bands. Today he brings the natural high of Pacific rainforests to jaded urbanites and manages to get them onside for the preservation of timeless natural wonders such as South Moresby in the Queen Charlotte Islands and the Carmanah Valley and Clayoquot Sound on Vancouver Island.

One hundred artists into the wilderness to create images of old-growth rainforest – that's the kind of project that appeals to Paul. In

1989 his environmental organization, the Western Canada Wilderness Committee (WCWC), employed this strategy in a bid to prevent the Carmanah Valley from suffering the clearcut logging that had been the fate of other coastal watersheds. "I think one of the real high points in my environmental work," Paul says in his WCWC office in Vancouver's Gastown, "was when the artists were all down at the camp on Carmanah Creek. I got there in the evening and all of these artists were talking around the campfire and comparing their sketches. A few had never been in an old-growth forest before."

The result of this elaborate undertaking – completed during four expeditions involving dozens of volunteers – was a book entitled *Carmanah: Artistic Visions of an Ancient Rainforest*, published by the WCWC, SummerWild Productions, and Raincoast Books. This spectacular art book won awards, raised public awareness, and made money for the fight to save the valley. "I'm sure the book was an important contributor to the creation of a park in the lower half of the valley in April 1990," says Paul, adding that funds from the book were also used to build a trail into the upper valley and to establish the world's first upper-canopy research station in a temperate rainforest. Work undertaken around that station has so far identified 500 new species of insects and arthropods, which in turn helped make the whole valley become part of the park in 1994. Contributing to the creation of a 14,826-acre park gives Paul great joy, but so do most things in life. A big, bearded man, he is a constant optimist. In another life he might have been a stock-market promoter, but in British Columbia he is revered, even feared, as a promoter of the preservation of Canada's wilderness.

The Carmanah project wasn't the first time Paul became involved in the promotion of artistic endeavours. In 1968 he was managing a psychedelic rock band at the University of Minnesota when the band's drummer was drafted. That event signalled the end of Paul's idyllic nine years on campus.

The band members began elaborate plans to get conscientious

objector status for the drummer. But as Paul explains it, the drummer was timid, succumbed to his parents' demands, and went off to war. "I got thinking about it," Paul recalls. "Here we had all these people dancing away with our multicoloured lights flashing and having a hell of a good time. And at the same time our boys were napalming these villages in Vietnam. It was just too schizophrenic for me, so we decided to take the whole band to Canada."

With a wife and three children, Paul was in no immediate danger of being drafted, but the reality of the war and what it was doing to American society was more than he could bear. "There was a real feeling of helplessness. It seemed like democracy was just falling apart. There was just no way you could even protest. A large percentage of the people were against the war, but if you went to participate in a demonstration, the viciousness of the people that you passed made you fear for your life. The pro-Vietnam War people were really scary."

In his university years Paul wasn't very politically active. However, he fondly recalls the time, in about 1965, when the House Un-American Activities Committee came to Minneapolis to hold hearings on a supposed plot to blow up the Mississippi River bridges during World War II. Paul demonstrated his opinion of the proceedings by carrying a kangaroo-shaped placard on a noose, an act that enraged his conservative countrymen.

Paul researched the planned exodus to Canada with full academic diligence. He studied the Canadian immigration system, which gave points for education, and realized that each band member would have no trouble gaining landed immigrant status. Not all of the band shared Paul's enthusiasm for Canada, though, and two of the members decided to apply only as visitors. Finally Paul was concerned that a whole band escaping the horrors of the American involvement in Vietnam might gain some media attention. He even suggested that the lead guitarist, Bill Smith, cut his long hair. Reluctant to do so, Smith compromised by stuffing his hair under a hat.

A convoy of five cars was arranged, carrying the band, members of their light show, girlfriends, and Paul's wife and children. In total there were 14 people travelling to Canada. Paul and his family went ahead of the others to the border crossing at Fort Frances, Ontario. Concerned that the whole convoy might be a bit overwhelming at the border, Paul had directed the vehicles to cross at half-hour intervals. Unfortunately Paul and his family were at the border longer than they had anticipated, and the car with Bill Smith arrived before they had cleared. In full paranoia, Paul and Bill pretended not to know each other and proceeded to ignore the familiar comments Paul's children exchanged with Bill. Luckily the border guards didn't catch on and declared everyone welcome to Canada.

Their research of Canada at the University of Minnesota had already identified Vancouver as the merry caravan's ultimate destination. None of the band had ever been to Vancouver, and they were in no great rush to get there now. They spent a leisurely two months camping their way across Canada, staying in federal and provincial parks.

At university Paul had studied math, chemistry, and biology and had taken sociology and psychology courses, as well. In the end, though, he completed a bachelor's degree with a double major in zoology and sociology. It was an ecology field course, however, that had contributed to Paul's unease about his future in the United States. He had lived on the Mississippi at Red Wing, Minnesota – about 60 miles south of Minneapolis – through much of his youth and had seen many changes in the environment. It was this course that gave definition to his newfound perceptions: "It did more to change my worldview than any other course I took. It had never occurred to me how much man had altered the natural environment. Each week we would go out to a rare remnant of a natural area and learn detailed ecological study techniques. One week it would be a maple-basswood forest, and another it would be savannah. Being on the edge of the prairie gave us quite a variety."

Another time the class was taken to a bog with an island of old-growth red and white pine that could only be reached by a board-walk. "I'd never seen trees like that," he recalls. "Someone named Lindeman, I think, had done some really fundamental work in defining ecology there. He had identified how much sunshine is coming in, what's happening to the energy, and how much is fixated by the photo plankton. The foundations of ecology were worked out there by this guy. Then we went on a three-day field trip up to Itaska State Park at the headwaters of the Mississippi River, and there was one of the largest extents of old-growth left. It was probably less than a square mile because the old-growth forests that had covered the Midwest had been almost completely liquidated by 1910."

The budding environmentalist cum rock band manager's love of parks blossomed in Canada. As the five-car convoy wandered across the country from park to park, Paul expanded his understanding of the beauty and complexity of the natural environment. "We went up to a park near Prince Albert in Saskatchewan. There was a lake there and we went on a hike around it. It was a hell of a hike. It must have been about 30 miles, and our poor lead guitarist lost his boots in a bog and he had to hike barefoot. We hit some wild areas in there and finally straggled back into camp after 15 or 16 hours. The guys in the band gave me the nickname Muckman and even wrote a song with that title. We all loved Canada. The people were really nice to us."

Paul led the troupe in his Nash Rambler onto Vancouver's psyche-delic West Fourth Avenue – Canada's equivalent of San Francisco's Haight-Ashbury – at the end of July 1968. It was the first time Paul had seen an ocean, and he fell in love with the peace-and-love scene in Vancouver and the beauty of the Spanish Banks. Shortly after arriving, they joined a group of people headed for the still-wild and isolated Long Beach on Vancouver Island's west coast. This was Paul's first exposure to the British Columbia rainforests that have been the focus of so much of his work. By way of introduction, it rained nearly every day on the Midwesterners at their Wreck Bay camp. Paul loved it: "We hiked the whole thing along trails that the Natives had used. We went down past their middens and saw huge whalebones."

In September they went back to the city to check out the music scene. The Poppy Family, with Susan and Terry Jacks, was the leading local band, but there was work for rock groups with good light shows. Paul began to line up a few gigs for the band, and they rented an old church for rehearsals. That fall of 1968 the students at the University of British Columbia (UBC) held a pub-in at their new student union building to protest the refusal of the authorities to allow a liquor licence on the premises. Paul's band, The Paisley Universe, played for the event.

Things were going well until the immigration people caught up with the two band members who hadn't become landed immigrants. "By Christmas time," Paul recalls, "all of the troupe had returned to the United States. As far as the band went, our debut up here was fairly short. The Paisley Universe reformed in the United States and continued as a very successful protest band throughout the balance of the Vietnam War."

In the sixties, alternative education programs flourished and Simon Fraser University opened its doors for the first time. The new university began offering a one-year teacher-training program for students who already had a degree and, with some financial help from home, Paul was able to enroll. The program involved extended practicums, and the following September Paul was placed at a junior secondary school in Richmond. "I really liked it. I was quite flamboyant in my teaching style," he says of those first teaching experiences.

Wanting to use his science background, he obtained an assignment on Vancouver Island that also put him closer to Long Beach. His sponsoring teacher at Nanaimo Secondary School was Ted Miller, who later became a Member of Parliament. After that he accepted his first, and his last, paid teaching assignment at Bellmont

Secondary School in Langford near Victoria. He stayed four years, then, on the day in 1974 that he became a Canadian citizen, he resigned. "I had gotten bored and I wanted to work with my hands."

Paul had already done a little carpentry rebuilding a house, and he was now ready to undertake larger projects. Soon he was involved in neighbourhood improvement plans in the Fernwood area of Victoria. He joined a neighbourhood organization to block off streets and create pocket parks. "I was becoming a Canadian. I wanted to be active and useful in Canadian society. This is where I was committed to stay and where my kids were growing up."

It was still an era when many people believed that with good intentions anything was possible. Paul still points with pride at neighbourhood improvements that resulted from that period. It was the early seventies, and along with his building work, he was commissioned to rewrite the provincial correspondence education course for grade 11 biology. The course would be mailed out to students in outlying corners of British Columbia, and Paul insisted that each student be supplied with a lab kit that included petri dishes and microscopes. In keeping with the era's hands-on discovery approach to education, Paul searched out local examples that students could be directed to in the various regions of the province. It was in so doing that he discovered an article in a 1974 issue of *Nature Canada* that told of the unique ecosystem of the Queen Charlotte Islands and advocated the preservation of South Moresby Island.

Paul was fascinated by the islands. He had met Richard Krieger, photographer and chess player, at one of the neighbourhood meetings. Together, the two bought a Zodiac inflatable boat and set off to explore the Charlottes. Their plan was to write a book. One of the places that they investigated was little Talunkwan Island at the mouth of Selwyn Inlet. The island was part of the larger Tree Farm Licence Number 24 (TFL 24), under which the provincial government granted a logging company the right to manage and harvest timber on a sustainable basis. Applying some of the ecology that he had learned back in Minnesota, and working with the figures laid out in the licence, Paul demonstrated that Talunkwan Island and the whole TFL was severely overcut. "I knew more about the TFL than the ITT-controlled Rainier Timber Company itself," Paul tells me. "I proved, using Talunkwan Island, that the whole TFL was at least 30 percent overcut. I saw how they scammed it. They would have the inventory show that there was so many cubic metres of wood in a particular cut block, then they would only scale out 70 percent of that. Next, they wouldn't subtract the overestimated portion so that even after they had logged 90 percent of the little 16-square-mile island, they would show that there was still seven years of old-growth to be cut there. Today about one-third of the whole island has eroded away because of the steep, unstable slopes. We called this kind of continued logging the 'talunkwanization' of South Moresby."

Paul made good use of his knowledge of biology, applying the years of expensive training that he had brought with him from the American university system. "The stupidity and blind arrogance of the foresters really angered me because they were wrecking the land and the salmon streams. They couldn't see what they were doing themselves because they had gone to the University of British Columbia for four years and had been brainwashed by a forestry department that taught mostly about how to log. That started me on a crusade that I am still on to get that profession on a scientific rather than a corporate ideology."

An American draft dodger, Tom "Huck" Henley, had joined with noted Haida activist Guujaaw and others to form the Islands Protection Society. Paul and Richard Krieger joined forces with the group and decided that the less-logged Lyell Island, inside the proposed South Moresby National Park Reserve, was the place to take a stand against the total destruction of Talunkwan. In 1975 Henley and Guujaaw collected 500 signatures to bring the issue to the attention of MLA Graham Lee, who was then a member of the short-lived NDP government. Later, in 1979, with hearings approaching for the renewal of TFL 24 under the new Forest Act, Paul prepared a detailed report on the overcut. Then he took his report to a faculty member in the Department of Forestry at UBC to substantiate his findings. While the professor agreed with Paul's figures and his methodology, he refused to sign an affidavit to the effect. He was concerned that he wouldn't get any more funding from the logging companies. "I was really furious," says Paul, "because I was brought up to believe that academically you had an obligation to be outspoken in expressing the truth."

Guujaaw and Chief Gnathion Young wrote letters detailing the damage to traditional Haida trapping areas on South Moresby and then went to court to stop the continued destruction. Paul George, Midwestern American biologist and rock band promoter, had found his niche. He became totally committed to the work of the Islands Protection Society and its fight to save South Moresby. "We knew that strategically that was the island that they were logging and it was some of the best old-growth left. I wrote up a proposal to make it an ecological preserve."

They succeeded in delaying any further logging and then presented themselves at the logging camp to put on a slide show illustrating the damages caused by this kind of activity. The show included shots of a 13-foot-diameter spruce with an eagle's nest that was cut down at the request of the Workers' Compensation Board because they feared it would fall on one of the camp's trailers. "This is the kind of ecological destruction that we don't like," they told the loggers, who sheepishly blamed the Compensation Board.

When Paul returned to Victoria to write his Queen Charlotte Islands book, he found himself too close to the subject and too removed from his family. The book project failed and his family fell apart, so Paul went back up to the Queen Charlotte Islands for another year and a half. In 1979 he worked with the Committee for Responsible Forest Legislation, lobbying for improvements to the new Forest Act. He saw this as an opportunity to pin the forest resource to its biological foundation. "I felt there absolutely had to be something about optimizing the flow and use of wood rather than maximizing the flow of fibre. But the act was railroaded through. It was just a sellout to the big companies and I was quite sick about it."

One of the last projects that Paul and his friends undertook in the Charlottes was the creation of a fact sheet on the wonders of the South Moresby National Park Reserve and how clearcut logging threatened it. The fact sheet came with a tear-off section at the bottom asking for funds to help save South Moresby. It worked really well, so they decided to do a calendar that, on a monthly basis, showed facts and a funding request for a different environmental group. They registered as a nonprofit organization, Richard Krieger mortgaged his house, and they printed 10,000 of the first Western Canada Endangered Wilderness Calendars. "Right from day one I've believed in the free enterprise aspect of it. There are too many government handouts. With my American background it just seemed to me that the government had their fingers everywhere. We decided to appeal directly to the people, but it was really low-key."

Paul also worked for three years as a researcher for the Nuu-chah-nulth Tribal Council and learned that there was more wilderness to be saved. During this time, as well, he expanded his understanding of the social injustices that First Nations are subject to in British Columbia. But by 1983 the Wilderness Calendar was in its third year and had gone into debt. It was time to grow or to die. Paul decided to stay with the Western Canada Wilderness Committee full-time. He and his new wife, Adrien, had just had their first baby, so Paul stayed home to care for the infant and run the wcwc from his house.

The wcwc has grown to become the largest preservation group in western Canada, with 15,000 active, dues-paying members and thousands of supporters. In 1995 the wcwc celebrated its 15th year of service with an impressive record of achievements in preserving old-growth rainforest. From time to time the environmental movement is criticized for being an elitist phenomenon, but Paul is proud that the wcwc has strong rural support through its chapters in Nanaimo, Nelson, and Kelowna. The organization has also fostered close alliances with First Nations and is currently working with the Lubicon people in Alberta to save the boreal forest there.

Now, as we finish up our talk in his office, Paul pauses for a moment, perhaps reflecting on the curious combination of circumstances that brought him to this Canadian metropolis at the edge of the rainforest. "I still feel different having spent my first 28 years in the States. As a first-generation Canadian, I can still feel like a foreigner when I go into the provincial legislature. I don't understand it as well as I should. In the United States we have the idea that if it's not illegal, it's legal. I think that too many times we don't recognize that the laws of life are above everything else. Once these ecosystems are gone, you never get them back. With social change a society always gets another chance. With ecological issues, when it's gone, it's gone."

RICHARD LEMM

Bard of Two Coasts

Dr. Richard Lemm, poet, associate professor, and past chair of the Department of English at the University of Prince Edward Island, came a long way before settling in the Maritimes. He now lives in Charlottetown, that small city where Confederation was first proposed in 1864, three years before Canada came into being. There was no flag waving or fireworks at the time, and no heroic speeches to commemorate the event. It was a quiet and somewhat staid occasion in a rather calm, unassuming place. More than a century later Prince Edward Island is, in many ways, still the same.

Richard didn't spend his childhood in the pastoral Prince Edward Island of *Anne of Green Gables*. Rather, born in 1946, he grew up on the opposite coast, in central Seattle, where he attended Franklin

High School, a short distance from Jimi Hendrix's Garfield High. The neighbourhoods served by Franklin High School spanned most of the socioeconomic spectrum, from the distinctly affluent families that lived along Lake Washington, through all levels of the middle class, to borderline poverty. Richard describes his immediate neighbourhood as being "what we called 'mixed,' and was later known as 'multiracial.' During the fifties it was mostly white – Italian, Anglo-Saxon, German, Greek – with some Japanese, Chinese, and Koreans, and a growing number of blacks. The racial mix shifted in the late fifties and early sixties until, when I was in high school, blacks were the majority in my neighbourhood."

Before enlisting to fight in World War II, Richard's father was a clerk at the *Seattle Times* in the days when men still did filing and typing. After his discharge, he worked for a movie distribution company, but was then killed in an automobile accident in 1947, less than a year after Richard was born. Richard's mother came from a Northwest pioneer logging family. Her husband's death was hard on her and she suffered a reactive depression which, in the late forties, was still treated with shock therapy and institutionalization. Richard was put in the care of his maternal grandmother, Aileen, who raised him with her second husband, Harry Osborn. Of his grandmother, Richard recalls, "She was the expressive and emotional one – a child of the logging camps. Even in her fifties, she loved to get all dressed up in black nylons and a black lace dress and go out for dinner at a tacky Chinese restaurant. She was a storyteller, and she permeates my whole being."

Aileen's emotive power inspired the poet in Richard, while Harry's strength helped him to define an independent, powerful identity. When Aileen died in Richard's 15th year, Harry became the sole parent by default. He taught Richard the fundamental American value of hard work: "He was a real survivor. He drove a taxi for about 10 years and then became a bartender. He was very good at what he did and he was a strong union man – the president of his branch of the Bartenders, Waiters, and Waitresses Union."

Richard was influenced by his grandfather's pro-union standpoint and came to understand the need to fight for the rights of the workers. But while Harry was a strong supporter of the working man, he was also of the pull-yourself-up-by-your-bootstraps school of social development. "My grandfather had a bit of right-wing populism in him, too," Richard recalls. "He was characteristic of the contradictions, or paradoxes, of the American union man: proworker but antisocialist. Back in 1964 he was set to vote for Barry Goldwater, but when he came out in favour of open shops, my grandfather deserted him for Johnson. Goldwater was great until he promised to break the unions."

While Harry upheld the rights of the common people, he was strongly opposed to the changes that were taking place in his neighbourhood in the late fifties and early sixties when more black families were taking up residence there. He insisted on staying in the neighbourhood long after most of his white neighbours had left, declaring that "no nigger is going to drive me out of my house." Richard recalls that "When it came to war, my grandfather believed in his president, 'right or wrong.' But when the Civil Rights Act was passed in 1964, he called Johnson a 'son of a bitch who ought to be impeached.'"

At the time that Richard attended Franklin High the student body was about 25 percent black, 10 percent Asian, and 65 percent white, including 10 percent Jewish. Because of this diversity, Richard's school was chosen by one of the major television networks to be the focus of a documentary on the American melting pot. They wanted to show "How wonderfully we all got along," Richard says wryly, pointing out that while there really was some legitimate mixing among the different ethnic groups, the television crews didn't go into the lunchroom where the various racial and social classes maintained a fairly high level of segregation.

But many of Richard's social ties developed out of his participation in sports. A self-declared jock, he lettered in both football and track. "There were a lot of heavy readers on the football team. Tom Gayton, our all-city ball carrier, is now a black activist peacenik who practises law in San Diego and has published two books of poetry. Don Gayton, no relation to Tom, was a lineman for our team and now lives in Canada, where he has published a beautiful book, *The Wheatgrass Mechanism*, on the prairie grasslands. Another starting lineman went to Vietnam and was so disillusioned with the United States when he came back that he moved to Australia and became a schoolteacher. It was a time when you could hang around with guys on the football team and discuss Plato and Bob Dylan and, of course, dance to James Brown, Ray Charles, and Stevie Wonder."

This eagerness to explore rich new ideas and experiences was as much a function of the period as of the place. It was a time of relative affluence, when populations and neighbourhoods were fluid with people who had experienced World War II and now felt freed from the social and economic constraints of those war years. Martin Luther King's voice was being heard everywhere and popular black music was getting airtime alongside the white artists on AM radio. The social activism of the thirties was still alive in spite of the best efforts of the House Un-American Activities Committee. And perhaps because Seattle is tucked into the Pacific Northwest, an even greater openness to competing ideas and movements was possible.

There were two places that Richard could go when things became difficult between him and his grandfather. One was the home of Bill Corr, Sr., the father of one of his high school friends: "He was one of the central working-class socialists in Seattle. The Corrs' house was a gathering point for older socialists and various Seattle activists. They had four sons, and I hung out at their house a lot."

While the library in Richard's grandparents' home featured authors like Zane Grey and Mickey Spillane, it was nevertheless extensive and he credits his family for his love of reading. "My grandparents weren't intellectuals, so at the Corrs' I was exposed to a whole new range of ideas and books. Bill Corr was of Irish stock and had been a longshoreman in New York. He had the scar to prove that he had been shot in the back during a strike on the docks. Bill forced people to confront their values and beliefs. When young people would toke up in his house, he would ask, 'What is that going to do for you intellectually and politically?' When I eventually decided to dodge the draft, he asked, 'Why? What are your methodological and ideological grounds for this decision?' He was a great teacher. He really made me think and he helped shape my identity a great deal."

Many years later Richard dedicated his poem "To an Old Socialist" to William Corr, Sr. In it he expresses his fondness and respect for the man:

> I admired how your carpenter's hands
> plucked open Lenin, or Sean O'Casey
> exactly at the page you wished to quote.
>
> I marvelled at the way you gathered friends
> and lonely strangers and troubled youth
> around your hearth, and opened their lives
> like vintage wine, like truth.

Richard's second refuge was at his friend Tom Gayton's house. It was here that he was exposed to music other than the rock and roll that he had grown up with in the fifties: "The black kids' parents were into older blues and jazz. By the time I was 16 I had spent many evenings sitting around with the Gaytons, listening to Billie Holiday, Duke Ellington, and Miles Davis. I spent much more time at their house than at my own during my last two years of high school. Mr. Gayton had been a jazz musician when he was young and knew a lot about music. He had a large record collection and many great stories to tell." But music wasn't the only thing that Richard was exposed to at the Gaytons'; he also became aware of "a whole other world – working-class black culture. This knowledge made me start to question the American system a lot more."

It was also Tom Gayton who made Richard conscious of the

extent to which white, middle-class, male values dictated aesthetic trends in American culture: "Some of my black friends were really down on black girls. They idealized white girls, especially blondes. I couldn't understand why they felt this way. Then Mr. Gayton pointed out that all the models and actresses, even the women in *Playboy*, who were the subjects of the average teenage boy's fantasy were white."

At one point in high school Richard began dating Sandra, the sister of one of his black friends. Sandra waited for him after football practice each day and they would drive down to the beach together, where Richard would help her with her homework. But interracial dating was quite uncommon at the time and his friends soon began to tease him about his relationship. In his poem "Before the Revolution," Richard recalls this painful experience:

> We keep playing at homework,
> my quick mouth, her alert
> silence. Dark in the car,
>
> she slides across the seat, hip
> touching mine. I could turn
> right toward the lake, the parking spots,
> but I can't. I go left toward her house.
>
> Away from the heat
> of her black skin and the
> words I know would come
> from DJ, the bloods on the block,
> if I stretched out, lowered my head,
> drove and scored
> so far from white.

With his growing awareness of issues around race and class leaving him almost totally estranged from his grandfather, Richard enrolled in his freshman year at the University of Washington in the fall of 1964. He struck up a friendship with his English teacher and her husband and began attending anti-Vietnam War rallies with them. Having left his friendly central Seattle neighbourhood behind, he found the campus up on the north side of town big and intimidating. With the war in full escalation, Richard began questioning his future and his moral stance on the draft. "I dropped out of university in December when my English teacher, who was supposedly my friend, gave me a final grade of C plus. I also felt very strongly that I couldn't morally maintain a student deferment now that the war was going on. I sent my deferment back to my draft board in pieces."

Reclassified 1-A, he applied for conscientious objector status. At age 18 he took a job as a clerk with the railway and decided that he would spend the rest of his life in blue-collar jobs and writing poetry. Turned down in his application for CO status, Richard began the appeal process. Changing addresses was a known way of stretching this process out, so he bought a car and set out to see America. From working-class bars in Pittsburg to an eastern farm at which Ginsberg was known to visit, Richard travelled the country and began to experience life in new and exciting ways. His travels also rekindled his interest in academics, and he enrolled at San Francisco State University while he continued to work on gaining an exemption from the draft. "I realized that eventually I would run out of appeals. I was visiting a couple up in Portland who I had met in my last year of high school, and they got me interested in returning to university."

Bob Grimm, a neurologist, and Nancy Grimm, a psychiatrist, introduced Richard to the world of highly educated professionals. Through the Grimms and their circle of friends Richard also became immersed in the worlds of backpacking and bird-watching, environmental activism, contemporary music, art, and endless, stimulating conversation. For Richard, "They embodied, and still do, everything wonderful in American liberalism – those values now threatened by the viruses spread by the Limbaughs and Gingriches of this world."

Bob was seeing a number of young men who refused to be drafted and were seeking medical deferments. Richard didn't consider this approach, but he was prepared to go to jail if he had to. The doctor dissuaded him from this option and explained that he could go to Canada instead. Richard protested that he couldn't possibly leave the States, but after a little more time in San Francisco and hearing from people who were going to Canada, he applied for the necessary papers. It was 1968, just before the point system for immigration to Canada was instituted. All you needed for acceptance was proof of employment and the ability to answer three questions on why you had left your native country and what your plans were for life in Canada.

One of his best friends from high school, Lance, had moved to Vanderhoof, a small logging and farming town in northern British Columbia, so Richard made his way there. Vanderhoof has a large First Nations population and, in the sixties, it was often considered Canada's racist equivalent of the American South. It certainly didn't celebrate its cultural diversity and it was a long way from San Francisco. Richard had only been there for a month, working at the St. Joseph Frontier Apostolate as a handyman, when Lance went back to Seattle to visit his father. "His father and some of his old high school friends guilt-tripped him about leaving the country," says Richard, "friends who were themselves getting out of the draft because they were in engineering school or their fathers had connections. So he enlisted in the navy for four years."

In the fall of 1969 Richard moved to Vancouver and got a job at Duthie Books. "Bill Duthie would never admit it, but by 1970 there must have been half a dozen draft dodgers working at his store. He would joke that we were all CIA agents planted in Canada. Sometimes he didn't need any staff, but he would hire people, anyway, just to provide them with a job letter. They would work three or four weeks and then he would say that they weren't needed anymore."

Later that year he enrolled at Simon Fraser University to complete his bachelor of arts. He graduated with an honours degree in English in 1971. While attending university, Richard lived in a beach house near the American border. It was to this house that his friend

Lance, looking like a wild man, returned, sporting a big black beard and hair down past his shoulders, and driving a Harley chopper. Lance had spent two years on a destroyer off the Vietnam coast. The ship's guns were automatically set to fire heavy artillery shells at shore targets around the clock day after day. There wasn't much to do on board, Lance explained, except drink and get stoned with the captain and crew. Lance eventually sold his Harley, bought a wooden sailboat, and lived at sea. His story ultimately served to confirm the choice that Richard had made – to live in Canada rather than to serve in Vietnam.

When Richard moved to Vancouver, he received a letter informing him that his appeal for conscientious objector status had been turned down and that there was a warrant out for his arrest on draft evasion charges. An RCMP detective visited him at his beach house. "He was extremely polite, which confirmed all of my impressions about Canadian cops. He asked if I intended to stay in Canada, and then he complimented me on my decision, my courage, and my principles. He said that if he had been in my place he would have done the same thing."

His fugitive status effectively meant that the border was closed to him and that he could no longer visit with friends and his grandfather in Seattle. His relationship with Harry continued to trouble him. In spite of his racist views, Harry had taught Richard to think critically of government and to question what he read in the newspapers and saw on television. This didn't make it any easier for the old man to accept Richard's move to Canada, but the two were beginning to write some good, long letters to each other. Richard was also in regular contact with his mother at the time. With the development of new drugs, her condition had much improved and she was beginning to spend more time at home.

After graduating from university, Richard found work in one of the Local Initiatives Programs that were set up to help young people and their communities in the early seventies. Richard's program trained lay therapists to work with kids who were experiencing failure in their lives. He liked the work and loved living in the Kitsilano area on Vancouver's west side, but he worried that he wasn't doing enough writing. "When I was 17 and 18 years old, I wrote a lot of fiction and poetry, but I was naive and sent my stories to *Playboy* and *Esquire.* I also sent my poems to *The New Yorker* and, of course, I got form rejection letters back. I was buying books by Nietzsche and Robert Frost rather than by contemporary Canadian authors who could have influenced my style."

Looking for direction, Richard took a course in poetry and creative writing from Al Purdy: "He used to go off to the pub with the whole class and, on the surface, I was so incensed with this irresponsible man that I stayed in the classroom and read poetry to myself. At a deeper level, however, I was still afraid of putting myself on the line as a poet or fiction writer. Back then bill bissett used to come into Duthie Books, but at the time I was too insecure as a writer to approach him. Today we're good friends."

In 1973 Richard discovered from some friends in Vancouver that the American government was beginning to drop charges against draft dodgers. Someone knew a lawyer in San Francisco who would research individual records for free. Richard contacted him and found out that the charges against him had been dropped in 1972 because he had been improperly denied conscientious objector status. This allowed him to travel in the United States once again, but his first experience crossing the border was nevertheless a stressful one: "The customs officer asked about my draft status during the war and I said, 'conscientious objector.' He punched this information into his computer and my heart was pounding in my ears. Then he looked at me and said, 'Have a nice visit.'"

In the summer and fall of 1974 Richard embarked on a rediscovery tour of his birth nation and wrote more poetry and plays. Within two weeks of returning to Vancouver, he had turned down several excellent job offers in order to concentrate fully on his writing. He settled back in Kitsilano to write, but there were just too many distractions. Fortunately, he met an American couple who lived in Hope, 100 miles up the Fraser Valley, and they invited him to live with them: "He was an ex-jazz musician turned haiku poet and tree planter. She was a preschool teacher."

Richard spent the next three years in Hope working as a substitute teacher and was able to do a lot of writing. "I started getting published in 1975 and began teaching a writers' workshop at the New Play Centre. That same year I was also hanging out with the Vancouver Poets' Co-op at the newly founded co-op radio. I also sat in on the Austin Pub Poets' Group with people like David Conn and Dave S. West. Some of that group are now part of the Vancouver Industrial Writers' Union."

In the summer of 1976 his wife, a doctor from New York whom he had met in 1972 and lived with since 1974, convinced Richard to go to the Banff School of Fine Arts to study with the likes of W. O. Mitchell, Alice Munro, and Eli Mandel. "I knew their names from Duthie Books, but at Simon Fraser I hadn't studied their work because there were no Canadian literature courses offered at the time. I went and got their books and was amazed at how good their writing was." The writing courses that Richard took in Banff had a profound effect on his life: "I thought, This is what I want to do. This is what I want to do with the rest of my life."

At the end of that summer Richard was asked to return to the school the following year as an assistant instructor. He also decided to undertake his master of arts degree, and enrolled at Queen's University in Kingston, Ontario, in 1978. After the summer of 1978, Eli Mandel, who had been head of poetry at the Banff School of Fine Arts, decided not to return, and Richard was appointed to the position in 1979. He continued teaching there every summer until 1986.

From 1978 until 1979 Richard lived and taught school in Ashcroft, British Columbia. During that year, he began to long for city life while his wife dreamed of a country house. They attempted to compromise by looking for a place on the Gulf Islands, but Richard's wife couldn't find a medical practice there and the land prices were far too high. Seeking to buy a farm, they travelled across Canada to the Annapolis Valley in Nova Scotia and purchased a piece of land there. Richard found work as a freelance resource journalist. His first article was on artificial insemination in beef cattle and earned him $50. He also applied to the local private school for a teaching position but began to worry again that he wasn't getting enough of his own writing done.

After two years he was offered a job by the private school and, at the same time, was granted a fellowship to do a Ph.D. at Dalhousie University in Halifax. He took the fellowship. His writing blossomed, he completed his doctoral course work and dissertation, and he published his first collection of poetry, *Dancing in Asylum,* in 1982. That year he and his first wife were separated and he moved to Prince Edward Island. After working as an editor with Ragweed Press, a small literary publisher in Charlottetown, he joined the faculty of the University of Prince Edward Island and eventually became chair of the English department. He then published two more books of poetry, *A Difficult Faith* (1985) and *Prelude to the Bacchanal* (1990). He has spent the past 10 years with his Canadian-born wife, the poet Lesley-Anne Bourne. Today Richard feels totally Canadian. Nothing about his citizenship is taken for granted. At the same time he recognizes his lack of Canadian roots and says, "I know that I will never fully be a Maritimer, and I never pretend to be anything that I am not. I feel lucky to have lived for a long time on both Canadian coasts and to have experienced, and been shaped by, their different cultures and landscapes."

Richard accepts and treasures his American origins, his West Coast background, and the role that his culturally rich Seattle neighbourhood played in shaping him and his poetry. He regrets that he and his grandfather never totally resolved their differences. They were becoming closer through their letter writing when Harry, still working in his seventies, was killed during a robbery at the bar. Later Richard learned that three black men had committed the crime. As they were leaving the bar, his grandfather called out defiantly, "You'll never get away with this, you niggers!" One of the men came back into the bar and shot him. The old ways die hard.

With proper medication Richard's mother was released from the hospital more than 30 years ago and is proud of her son's accomplishments in Canada, particularly his literary ones. His ability to connect with people of various socioeconomic backgrounds and his experience of having lived on American and Canadian soil, and on both the east and west coasts, have provided Richard with much of the imagery, insights, and observations of which his poetry is made. But Richard Lemm has contributed to Canadian culture not only as a fine poet and an accomplished academic, but as an inspiring example of perseverance. Growing up without parents, suffering the loss of his grandmother, and then enduring a painful estrangement from his grandfather, Richard has not only carried on, he has done so with great tenacity and incredible success.

JOHN SHINNICK

Soldier of Peace

THERE HAVE BEEN times in John Shinnick's life when people have called him "Tex" and expected him to know all about cows. But John didn't grow up in the Texas of wide-open plains and vast ranches. Rather, he grew up in East Texas, the son of a Cajun mother who spent her younger years on a houseboat in the bayous of Louisiana while her father worked as a shrimper. Eventually her family relocated to Orange, Texas.

Orange, a town with a population of about 25,000 today, as it was in the fifties, sits on the Sabine River, which forms the boundary between Louisiana and Texas, and on the edge of the bayou swamp country that stretches eastward along the Gulf of Mexico to the mouth of the Mississippi. John's maternal grandfather, Ben Veazey, built and fished Gulf Coast shrimp boats out of nearby Cow Bayou. "English was a second language to my grandparents," recalls John. "My great-grandmother spoke no English whatsoever, only French. My grandfather was full of stories. He was a classic Cajun shrimper who also ran a bootleg operation back in the bayous in the twenties during Prohibition."

When I first met John in the late eighties, he was an editor with *Pacific Yachting* in Vancouver. He told me that he and his wife lived aboard a powerboat moored at the stylish, yuppie False Creek Yacht Club, but I didn't know that he was following in the marine tradition of his mother's Cajun family. Another interest that he inherited from his mother was photography.

Somehow John's mother had been able to leave the conservative confines of Southern womanhood to travel north to photography school in New York City during the forties. Throughout John's childhood she operated a small photography studio in Orange. "I sometimes think my mother was a fairly liberated woman given the times," John says, recalling the Cleaver family model on the popular television series *Leave It to Beaver*. "She and my father split up when I was 16. It was a very traumatic experience for her, and I don't think we ever really appreciated who she was, what she did, and what she wanted to do with her life. In the fifties and sixties women weren't carrying on careers, and that was something she really wanted. But we all wanted a June Cleaver, stay-at-home type of mom, like our friends had."

John's father had grown up a North Dakota farm boy in a German-Irish family. He went into the army during World War II, flew dozens of B-17 bomber missions over Germany, and then served in the air force reserves until his retirement. After settling in Orange with his wife, John's father worked for Allied Chemical as a mechanical engineer, but always stayed active in the reserves. Most summers John travelled with his family to bases throughout the United States until his parents split up in 1963.

John attended Catholic school until the sixth grade when his younger sister was beaten up by a nun and his father put them into the public school system. John graduated from Luther Stark High School in 1965. The school was segregated but, by the time John's sister went there, it had become integrated, in keeping with the more tolerant times. John still gets upset when he recalls the vicious segregation that was enforced in East Texas. "Even the churches were segregated," he recalls. "I have this memory of being in St. Mary's Catholic Church on a beautiful, sunny Sunday morning when a black girl came to mass. It was the first time it had ever happened, and these white women got up and stormed out of the church in a huff. I have always wondered about that girl. It took an amazing amount of courage to walk into that church. Who was she? Where did she come from? Where did she go after that?"

John has other memories of the racist horror that was a day-to-day fact of life in Orange. "There was a garage right next door to my mother's photography studio. When I was about 12 years old, I hung out there with all the mechanics and the people who would come in to have their cars fixed. The police brought their cars there, and I remember watching these officers and some other people bully a black guy one day. They put handcuffs on him, threw him into the back of a police car, and told him they were going to turn him over to the local Ku Klux Klan."

When they had had their perverse fun, they threw the weeping man out into the street. John's face is contorted with horror and revulsion as he recalls the event: "This man was a human being who had been driven to tears because, as far as he knew, he was going to be castrated, or tarred and feathered, or lynched, and these men thought it was a big joke. The Klan had this sort of presence in the town and that presence is still there. It is one of the reasons I would never go back and live there."

John was 16 when the young black girl bravely walked into his church. He was beginning to hear a little about civil rights, but acknowledges that he wasn't completely politically aware yet. "When I was 16 or 17 years old, I actually told my dad that I wanted to go to Vietnam and fly a helicopter. I thought it would be a great thing to do." In spite of, or perhaps because of, his World War II military experience, John's father told him, "You're crazy. You didn't start that war. Your generation didn't start that war. You certainly shouldn't have to go and fight it."

The idea and ideals of justice were central to John's training as an American: "Justice was an American concept as far as I was concerned." Reflecting on it today, he says, "Justice was ingrained in who we were. We took the Pledge of Allegiance in school every morning, and I remember the phrase 'and justice for all.' I still believe it is an incredible concept. Look at these nutcases who really want to tear the country apart – like the bloody militia guys who blew up the Federal Building in Oklahoma City in 1995. Rabid nationalists are doing it in the name of the Constitution and justice, but the only justice they want is justice for their greed, not justice for all human beings. Ronald Reagan let these people feel very smug and comfortable in their prejudices."

John remembers the incredible poverty and institutionalized racism of the South, and wonders both about his acceptance of it at the time and his good fortune in having escaped the narrow confines of that world. "It wasn't until I left there and then went back that I came to understand the underpinnings of that society. No matter what anybody says about racism in Canada, it is not officially condoned. Down there it was the law. If your skin was a different colour, you had no rights."

John entered Lamar University in Beaumont, Texas, in September 1965. He studied engineering but changed disciplines several times in that first year. The university wasn't very far from his home and the values weren't all that different, but he began to see some cracks in the rigid Southern codes. "I can remember going to some of the early National Association for the Advancement of Colored People's rallies down there, and the change was coming even though nobody wanted to acknowledge it." Still, John admits, "It was as backward as you can get as far as mainstream politics go. There was no talk of the civil rights or antiwar movements. I didn't know any of this was even happening until I joined the Peace Corps."

It was the Peace Corps that gave John his first real taste of life outside of the confines of the South. "One of the reasons for being in university at that time was to avoid the draft. That was a sort of privilege. My grades were good enough and my father could afford to send me to university. But an alternative was the Peace Corps, which was a fascinating thing. I remember seeing these commercials on late-night television showing people working in villages with oxen. I was intrigued. I phoned the number and got the information."

Many of John's friends were leaving university to go to Vietnam – a few of them with the "kill a Commie for Christ" fervour that seems strange today, but was only too real in 1967. Unsure of what he wanted to study, but knowing that he didn't want to go to Vietnam, John dropped out halfway through his second year at Lamar and enlisted in the Peace Corps. It was not only a means to avoid the draft and see the world, but an opportunity to meet people who read a little more broadly than the folks in Orange, who were devout readers of Mickey Spillane, Leon Uris, Harold Robbins, and Ian Fleming. "It wasn't until I got into the Peace Corps that I learned what good writing was all about. Part of our equipment was a box of books for a library. I was introduced to a broader spectrum of literature. I read Ken Kesey's *One Flew over the Cuckoo's Nest*. I read Joseph Heller's *Catch-22* 13 times. I read John Updike, Anthony Burgess, and Jack Kerouac. In the two years that I was in the Peace Corps I read eight or 10 books a month."

But before the government let a Southern white boy go off to Africa, they gave him some basic training and checked that his American values wouldn't prove too embarrassing, or offensive, in a foreign country. After gathering with other potential recruits in

Philadelphia, John was sent to Frogmore, South Carolina, where he boarded with an African-American family. "The Peace Corps was the best thing that I ever did," John recalls. "I have a picture of me and my partner the day that the two of us were taking off for the bush of Gabon. It shows me as a 19-year-old kid who is *so* arrogant. You couldn't tell that kid anything. He had the whole world figured out and he was going to go and build schools."

Over the next several months John and his group did build a school in Luango to replace a thatched hut that the community had used up until then. But they didn't get to finish the building. In 1967, after seven months and 15,000 bricks, John and his group made a three-day, 70-mile trip to spend Christmas in the coastal village of Mayumba when a Peace Corps organizer arrived by plane. He brought word that the Corps had been expelled and they had 24 hours to get out of the country. The group made a quick trip back to Luango to retrieve their belongings. The adventure of getting out of the country, including a flight to the capital of Libreville on an over-loaded DC-3, made a big impression on the young Americans. They were caught up in international politics driven by France and the United States, and felt the pressure of African soldiers with Sten guns who had no love for America. John revisited the country in 1994 and the trip confirmed his feeling that, "No matter what they did to me in West Africa, it could in no way approach what happens to a black person in America. They accepted me, they sometimes treated me a little strangely, but they certainly didn't treat me as though I were some kind of inferior being."

John spent a couple of months in Sierra Leone looking for a new assignment. He was repeatedly asked to work on livestock projects because of his Texas origins. Eventually a rural development opportunity opened up in Senegal, and he went to work there for the next 15 months to complete his tour of duty. He spent the summer hitch-hiking on freighters down the coast of Africa and then travelled by train back up through the interior. By the time he left West Africa, he had visited 25 countries and learned to communicate in five languages. At 21 he was a very different person than the one who had left East Texas two years earlier.

"I sort of lost myself in West Africa," John says now. "I still didn't know what I wanted to do. I did know that I wanted to write, but I had forgotten how to speak English. I got hold of a copy of the Perrin-Smith handbook of English and started teaching myself grammar. I approached my own language the same way I had approached French and the other languages that I had learned."

John headed home by ship via the Canary Islands, Spain, Portugal, France, and Luxembourg. He flew to the Bahamas and spent his last $30 on a plane ticket to Miami. From there he hitch-hiked back to Texas, arriving unannounced in his hometown. John walked into his father's carport and found him working on the family car – a kind of Norman Rockwell, son-home-from-his-travels picture. Small-town America showed no apparent change, but John had changed irrevocably. In the Peace Corps he had met other workers with degrees from such places as MIT, the University of Southern California, and Berkeley. He had travelled with young people from other countries, including a young French Canadian in the summer of 1968, who got him thinking about moving to Canada as an alternative to the draft. While his father was somewhat accepting of his new ideas, John says ruefully, "My mother accused me of having been strapped down on a table and brainwashed by the Communists. Despite the fact that she had voted for Democrat Adlai Stevenson in the fifties, she was a card-carrying John Bircher and thought Richard Nixon was a pinko."

John got more politically involved when he went back to Lamar University in 1969. "I got tired of the lies," he recalls. "I had a history professor who was giving us the line about how the Chinese hordes were going to overrun South Vietnam. I pointed out to him that the United States had 500,000 troops in South Vietnam and that nobody had ever heard of 500,000 Chinese troops there. In any case, the Vietnamese didn't want the Chinese anywhere near them. What bugged me the most was that there were people teaching who had these kinds of agendas."

There were, however, a few like-minded people on campus, and John drew support from them. He became involved with a student group that published an underground newspaper. "That's where I did some of my earliest writing. Because I had been separated from Texas culture for two years, I had some perspective."

Compared to the kind of antiwar activities that were taking place at Berkeley in 1969, the campus in Beaumont was pretty subdued. "Down in Texas, 'radical' was totally middle-of-the-road. We belonged to a splinter group of the Democratic Party called Students for Democratic Action. It was committed to integration and an end to the Vietnam War." But John still felt that he wasn't doing enough, and by the fall of 1969 he knew he had to make a change. He had also come to realize that he was benefitting from racial and economic privilege by using his student deferment as a means to avoid the draft. "There was a preponderance of young black guys my age who were being forced to go and die, and I was having a hard time living with that. I knew I would have to leave."

That summer John had become engaged to Judy, a friend from his high school years. They married in the fall of 1970 and headed for the Pacific Northwest. Judy had a teaching degree from Lamar but, except for visits to Louisiana, she had never left Texas. They were heading for Canada, but stopped in Washington State for a couple of months to see if John's number would come up in the draft lottery. His number did come up, and he was ordered to report for induction on February 27, 1970. He and Judy crossed the border into Canada on February 26. "I had nightmares for a long time after that and would wake up screaming. I would see footsteps coming across the bed to get me. It was quite a while before those dreams went away."

They entered Canada as visitors and applied for landed immigrant status from within the country. The French that John had learned in the Peace Corps gave him as many points in the immigration process as a university degree. The couple didn't know anyone in Canada, but they rented a little house a short distance from the border at Crescent Beach in White Rock, British Columbia.

John's first real job in Canada was with Dave Dunn at CKOV Radio in the Okanagan, where he wrote ad copy for a couple of years. He then left the radio station to begin work on his own novel. In 1978 John honed his writing skills and his awareness of Canadian letters at the Banff School of Fine Arts, where he studied creative writing under such literary mentors as W. O. Mitchell and Sylvia Fraser. Later he went back to the radio station as creative director and then moved on to FM radio. Judy was working as a teacher at the time, and the couple made a lot of friends among the many young people who were working in the Canadian media. In 1982 John was successful in his application for the assistant editor's position at *Pacific Yachting*, the glossy publication serving West Coast recreational boaters. He and Judy moved to the coast, bought their dream boat, and lived on board throughout John's 13 years as assistant, and then full, editor of the magazine.

Because John had taken the military physical with the draft board in 1965, he was designated a felon when he left the United States to come to Canada. The FBI paid regular visits to his parents. John's mother, who was convinced that her son had become a Communist, was glad to have someone to talk to about it. John's father, on the other hand, was always courteous to the officers, but he just wanted to know if his son was all right. In 1974, when John and Judy were still living in the Okanagan, they received phone calls from the FBI on a regular basis, wanting to know if John would partake in the clemency program that was sponsored by President Ford. It was conditional on two years of alternative service. The FBI said, "All you have to do is go down across the border and work in a hospital for a while." To which John, like many other draft evaders, replied, "I have done nothing wrong. I did exactly what my conscience told me to do, and

I'm not going to apologize or do penance for it."

In 1977 President Carter's amnesty allowed John to travel in the United States to do some writing; ironically, for the government-funded U.S. Travel Service. John followed his dreams again when, in 1995, he left *Pacific Yachting* to take over ownership of another magazine, *Media Wave* – an innovative presentation of the Tofflerian era of communications. The greater part of the magazine is put together electronically in the corner of John and Judy's apartment. The Internet allows John to travel the world at home, selecting graphics and text to download for inclusion in each issue. It also serves as a means of connection. While I had known John for several years, I didn't realize he was a draft evader until I posted a bulletin on an electronic newsgroup looking for people to interview for this book. John responded. In so many ways then, John is typical of the many Americans who came to Canada during the Vietnam War. They have fitted themselves into the stream of Canadian society so completely that their compelling and courageous stories can elude even a native-born individual, like myself.

ROGER DAVIES

And Justice for All

"AN UNDERLYING SENSE of social justice" is the first idea that comes to Roger Davies's mind when asked about his parents. "Not that my parents were radical social activists," he says. "In fact, my father was a registered Republican earlier in his life, but has been voting Democratic for some time now. He wasn't motivated by greed as so many Republicans are today, though. He just believed that small businesses and institutions would fare better with more restricted government involvement in economic life. I remember him showing me some information in the fifties that demonstrated that an American worker laboured far fewer hours to buy a pair of shoes than a worker in Russia. To him, this was somehow proof that we had a better system. There was never any discussion of health care, education, or any issues like that."

We are sitting at the kitchen table of the modest bungalow that he shares with his wife, Judith. His grown daughter, Gwyneth, lives with her partner in a basement suite, in keeping with what seems to be the prevalent style of the nineties. The house is in a quiet neighbourhood in Halifax, Nova Scotia, and a long way from Cleveland, Ohio, where Roger's father was the president of the North American Manufacturing Company, a firm that produced heating equipment and hydraulic controls.

Roger's parents were married in 1937. They suffered through the Great Depression and then endured the Second World War, although Roger's father was never called to serve because his work, which was considered militarily significant, exempted him. For many Americans, the plenitude of the fifties was seen as a just reward for the two previous decades of restraint. Roger's family had a fine house in Shaker Heights, the wealthy area of town. He attended a good public school at a time when funding for education, particularly in the suburbs, was seen as a priority. But even Shaker Heights wasn't excluded from the prejudice and discord of the fifties.

"America promised its citizens the democratic ideal of freedom and justice for all. I think I was always somewhat cognizant of the disparity between that ideal and the reality," Roger reflects. He recalls "having a black friend named Edwina Johnson in elementary school and encountering racism for having that friendship. I had it in my mind that Edwina should visit my home. She did visit me one afternoon, and at the dinner table that night there was a joke made by my sisters about 'Roger having a little black girl coming to visit.' It was considered kind of funny, but not in a malicious way. My parents didn't quite know what to do and they didn't say much, but the message that there was something wrong with having her over got through to me."

Racial divisions learned in elementary school were coupled with class tensions in high school. "Most of the kids in my high school went to university, but there were those who couldn't afford to and went to trade schools instead. This was the time of the 'greasers,' when certain types of clothing identified class differences." Although racism and classism were not things that were discussed at home or in school, Roger had developed a clear sense of them by the time he graduated from high school in 1963. However, it would be some time before he came to understand how these issues related to war.

Like so many young people, the only knowledge Roger had of war was what he learned through games and television. "I would play war quite a bit with the neighbourhood kids. We would have these extended battles with our toy rifles. As a 10-year-old, I watched *Airpower* and *Victory at Sea* and all the television shows that depicted war. I had a sense that it was a bad thing, but I also had a feeling that it might have been heroic for my father to have fought in World War II rather than having stayed at home to work. So, in 1958, when we visited my sister's first husband at the naval academy in Annapolis, I thought it was all pretty neat. But I also recall seeing how he looked and hearing how he spoke – I was picking up on the regimentation and dehumanization of it all – and I recognized the loss of individuality that was required in the face of authority. In the eyes of a 14-year-old, he was just becoming part of the machinery."

Roger credits this early questioning of conventional masculine roles to his mother. Born and raised in a Unitarian family in Evanston, Illinois, Roger's mother brought a sense of the arts and an appreciation of things beyond the material to her family. She had studied Greek, Latin, and English at liberal Oberlin College and played the piano beautifully. She intuitively conveyed to Roger "that the world of men can be driven to harsh and violent extremes that must be avoided."

This redefinition of the male role has become more important to Roger as he approaches the end of his 50th year. He has read the works of poet Robert Bly and a host of other writers on masculine identity. He has participated in male support groups that serve to develop one's ability to nurture others and share grief. He identifies a strong link between these ideas and his improved relationship with his father: "My father died in the fall of 1995, but in the year before that we had gotten on track, he at the age of 83 and me at the age of 50. But there were many years when we had a lot of trouble communicating."

In the fall of 1963 Roger enrolled at DePauw University in Greencastle, Indiana. "It was the wrong university for me," he now sees. "It was a highly conservative Midwestern school. Both of my sisters had gone there and I just kind of fell into it. I joined a fraternity that turned out to be pretty racist. There was quite a contrast between the kind of fraternity and sorority stuff that was happening on campus and the things that were beginning to happen in the country."

Kennedy was assassinated in November of Roger's first year, but he recalls no political analysis of the event. He was even discouraged by one of his professors to join the civil rights Freedom Riders on their trek to Alabama. He sees all of this as a pervasive inertia and an unquestioning support of the status quo. In retrospect, Roger sees that his high school in Shaker Heights did more to stimulate critical thought than the anti-intellectual environment of DePauw, where social life took precedence over social issues.

He did, however, manage to find pockets of like-minded people at DePauw. He had planned to go to medical school but, because he had difficulties with chemistry, he decided to study philosophy instead. In this department he found a socially concerned professor, Dr. Compton. "The place where we connected was around ethical inquiry and making your beliefs become real. In 1966, when I was in my third year, I became part of a group that organized a trip to the Detroit ghetto to try to understand what was going on there. This was the year before the Detroit riots and people were telling us that the city was going to blow. I remember one speaker there drawing a parallel between America's treatment of people in Detroit's inner city and their treatment of the Vietnamese. That kind of analysis blew my mind. Old Dr. Compton was the only prof that would sponsor us to go, and he gave up his spring break to join us in sleeping bags on the floor of a church basement."

Throughout his four years of university, Roger's knowledge of political issues and world events progressively increased. By his third year he had moved out of the fraternity house and had rented an apartment. An awareness of what was going on in the country was beginning to seep into DePauw. He and six others formed a tiny local chapter of Students for a Democratic Society. One of their first actions was to organize a protest against a military recruiting drive on the campus. "I remember growing a sixties-style, 'political' mustache that year. There is a lot to be said for placing yourself in opposition to the system, but it would have been nice to be among even more people with the same goals," he says wryly.

In the summer of 1966, following his third year, Roger joined the migration to California to attend summer classes at Berkeley. "I met people there who were actively engaged in stopping the war and were blocking the troop trains at Oakland." He also got involved in a tutoring program for black kids and continued that work when he returned to DePauw in the fall of that same year.

But Roger found that the campus scene back in Indiana was still entirely withdrawn from what was happening in the country, so he dropped out of school and went to New York City. He found an apartment in Greenwich Village and then later moved to the East Village. He worked at a mail-order house in order to pay the bills, and moved in with a woman he met in the city. Setting up a darkroom, he began to pursue his interest in photography and started attending poetry readings. Roger was now well launched on a path to self-discovery, using photography and poetry as vehicles to take him there.

Like many contemporaries, he participated in antiwar demonstrations in Times Square and went to Washington to picket the White House. His New York sojourn lasted a year, during which he took a couple of courses at Columbia University, returning eventually to DePauw to complete the necessary course work for his degree.

After completing his final semester, Roger received his draft notice, which came as no surprise. He began to think that perhaps a club-foot that had been successfully operated on at birth might qualify him for a medical exemption. He took the bus from Newcastle, Indiana, to Indianapolis with a bunch of other young men called up for their medical exams. They sang Arlo Guthrie's great song "Alice's Restaurant," with its all too relevant lyrics about a young man attempting to fail his physical. But Roger passed the physical and, sometime later, received a letter telling him where to report for induction.

He had already considered his four options: to go underground, to become a conscientious objector, to go to jail, or to move to Canada. Roger found the last option the most appealing. He had vis-ited Quebec City and had attended summer camps in Ontario when he was young, "so Canada had this romance about it. A place with the beautiful, wide-open wilderness and intriguing cities. I had a sense that Canada would be good for me and I would be good for Canada."

Although initially bewildered, his parents were supportive of his decision and helped with the practical matters of the move. Within a few days Roger was across the border and in Canada. Remembering the crossing of the 21-year-old boy, who had felt himself on the out-side for much of his life, still brings tears of emotion to the eyes of the 50-year-old man. "I remember being made to feel really at ease. The immigration officer shook my hand and welcomed me to Canada without asking why I had come. When I think about the massive force that was prepared to turn me into a killer for no good reason and then this incredible warmth and understanding, I am still over-whelmed."

Having received some draft counselling from a group of Quakers in Bloomington, Illinois, Roger immediately contacted the Union of American Exiles in Toronto, who arranged a place for him to stay. The Quakers had also told him about the option to renounce his cit-izenship before the date on which he was to report for induction. He enrolled to start a teacher's training course in the fall and arranged to meet with the American consulate. "They were quite concerned about my decision and asked, 'Are you sure you want to do this? Do you know what rights you will be giving up?'" But Roger could not be dissuaded. He completed the necessary papers and then sent his draft board proof of his renunciation of his American citizenship. "I had no reply from them and the date of my induction came and went. Then I got a letter from the government saying that I had committed an offence."

This seemed to be the last straw for Roger's Republican father, who was now totally disenchanted with the obvious duplicity of Nixon's government. An important part of Roger's father's political shift from the Republican to the Democratic Party came from ideas and ideals that he had learned from his son. Now, when Roger was being pursued by the draft board of a country to which he was no longer affiliated, his father offered support. "He got a good lawyer who straightened everything out. I was legally correct. You can't draft someone who is not a citizen of your country."

Roger took to Canadian life with a passion. After completing his teacher's training course, where he met his wife, Judith, he applied for, and got, a job at Musgrave Harbour in Newfoundland. Leaving Judith behind in her job as an editor at Macmillan Publishing, Roger bought a Land Rover and drove east. Rural Newfoundland came as a shock to him. "It was fascinating. Early on in the first year I tried to teach things that I had taught in Toronto, like the poetry of Allen Ginsberg. The students tolerated me, and it turned out to be a learning experience for both them and myself."

When a permanent elementary school position opened up, Judith joined him in Newfoundland. They were married and then had their daughter, Gwyneth. They bought a fisherman's house for $600 and learned to sleep while winter storms shook the structure to its foundations. "I was struggling with septic systems. We had a wood stove that provided barely enough heat. I would wake up in the morning and the water in our little washbasin would be frozen. It was a sort of semi-back-to-the-land experience. I read the *Whole Earth Catalogue!*"

After four years in Newfoundland, the young couple began to crave a more urban setting. Roger wanted to pursue his interest in photography further and they were starting to think about their daughter's schooling. Consequently they moved to Halifax, where Roger enrolled in art school. He has since taught in a variety of school settings, including an alternative school for at-risk youth and nine years doing an educational program in a correctional centre. He is now coordinating adult literacy programs at two Halifax libraries, a continuation of the work that he started with Oakland inner-city kids the summer that he spent at Berkeley. He has also worked to develop an antiviolence curriculum for junior high schools. With violence in schools becoming a growing issue throughout North America, the curriculum has been widely received and is now being used in schools in Miami, among other urban centres.

Roger nurtures his appreciation of life with his spiritually inspired nature photography and his 22-foot dory, which he sails out of Mahone Bay. The Universalist-Unitarian Church, the same church Roger's mother was brought up in, provides him and his wife with a source of strength and a haven of community. In recent years Roger has been paying regular visits to the United States to see his parents and his sisters. Through his church, his family, and his work he has explored a wide range of issues concerning masculinity, violence, and the freedom to grieve and express emotion. Roger has met the challenges of life in his new country and, in so doing, the original assumption on which he relocated – that Canada would be good for him and he would be good for Canada – has been proven several times over.

MARY CLEEMPUT

Of Home and Holography

As she stands in her walk-up apartment, Mary Cleemput's open expression and wheat-blond hair speak of her youth as a Midwestern farm girl. The journey from country girl to internationally known holography artist has been a long, and at times difficult, one for Mary, but nothing has dulled her modestly expressed enthusiasm for life. Having raised her children, she is now following her art wherever it takes her. In the late eighties, when her son and daughter both graduated from high school, she sold her house in Toronto and left her nursing career behind. After she moved to Montreal and then New York, Mary's prominence in the world of art holography increased and eventually she decided to settle in Vancouver in 1993. Today she lives on Commercial Drive, located in Vancouver's east end. She loves the mix of working-class immigrants – mostly Italian – and the artists that share and contribute to the neighbourhood known locally as "The Drive." Much of Mary's art reflects the lively street scene of people and sidewalk markets that extends up and down this bustling East Side street.

Mary is comfortable with moving around now, but in 1969, when she first followed her husband north to Canada in his effort to avoid the draft, it was a much more traumatic experience. Born in Ohio, the third girl in a family of eight children, Mary had a classic Midwestern, conservative upbringing. Her father had emigrated from Belgium, going first to Canada, and then, as an itinerant worker, to the United States. "He told us that he had gone to Canada first to avoid being drafted into the Belgium army," Mary says. As an unskilled factory worker, her father's outlook was simple: "We came to this country with nothing, and now we own a farm."

Life only got better for Mary when, as valedictorian of her high school graduating class, she went off to Ohio State University and became a nurse. "I was very conservative, having come right off the farm. I remember when Pete Seeger came to sing at OSU, my roommate and I sat in the front row and refused to applaud. I was dating a John Bircher from Toledo at the time, and he believed all those hippie types were part of a Communist conspiracy to undermine our great nation."

A year later Mary met and married a medical student from Dublin, Ireland, whose background and politics were quite different than her own. Born to an American father and an Irish mother, both physicians themselves, he spent his childhood in Dublin and in Wisconsin, never quite feeling that he fitted into either place. As a child he attended a strict Jesuit boarding school and later studied medicine in Dublin. He and Mary met in Columbus at a hospital where he was working for the summer. "He was a compassionate physician and he introduced me to Joyce and Rilke. Of course I fell for him." After his graduation from medical school back in Ireland, the couple married, and within two weeks of his return to the United States, he began his internship in Syracuse, New York.

Upstate New York seemed like the perfect place for this young intern, whose politics were somewhat leftist from having grown up in Dublin. It was the time of Woodstock and the Peace and Freedom Party, with Eldridge Cleaver running for president. The Women's Liberation Movement was gaining momentum, and strong leaders in the National Organization of Women came from the ranks of middle-class professionals. Twenty-year-olds were reading Herbert Marcuse and Noam Chomsky and quoting from Mao's *Little Red Book*. But it was 1969 and the new young doctor was contacted by his draft board almost immediately. When his first year's internship was finished, he would be inducted. "There really was no questioning our decision to leave. He had American citizenship but felt no loyalty to the country. He didn't want to spend three years in someone else's war. Furthermore, I was pregnant with our first child and didn't relish the thought of raising a family alone at age 24."

The couple's friends supported their decision to go to Canada, where a position at McGill University in Montreal awaited Mary's husband. The young doctor's father also encouraged the move, but Mary was unprepared for the reaction that she received from her own family and friends back in Ohio. It wasn't easy for Mary to leave them behind, and it was hard for her parents to watch their daughter, who they had always been so proud of, leave her country. Mary believes that her mother still hasn't told some of her brothers and sisters why her daughter and her doctor-husband went to Canada. At the time, she wrote Mary a disapproving letter, saying, "He is a doctor and it is his duty to serve his country. He should be in Vietnam helping the wounded." Even Mary's closest friend from her nursing days voiced similar disappointment. When Mary crossed the border, she made some very deep cuts in her ties to her family and friends.

It was June 1969 when the couple moved to Montreal, and not long after the RCMP called to see if their papers were in order. There was likely some contact between the American and Canadian authorities, but the couple's papers were satisfactory and the RCMP didn't bother them anymore. However, the American military didn't give up on potential medical officers so easily. "Over the next few years the FBI called on every member of my family," Mary recalls. One of her younger sisters had a secretarial job with the FBI in Washington. "They threatened to have her fired from her job. They demanded to know where we were. They had all that information. It was merely intimidation. Then an agent went to the farm in Ohio and informed my father that it was his duty to turn in his son-in-law if he ever returned. They overstepped a line there, and my family began to change its attitude about what we had done."

Mary's father was patriotic, she explains, but he was also an American who didn't believe that the government should be interfering in family matters in this way. "He stood up to them," Mary says with pride. "He believed in law and order and the goodness of America, but he said, 'You cannot ask me to do that – that would be wrong.'"

In spite of the FBI's attempts to make their lives miserable, the young refugees settled down in Montreal, where their first child, a daughter, was born in 1969, followed by a son in 1971. Both children had the opportunity to be American as well as Canadian citizens, but Mary didn't register their births with the American consulate. "We didn't want our children to be subjected to the American draft and to have to go through what we had."

With problems already beginning to develop in their marriage, the young family moved to Newfoundland, where Mary's husband got a temporary position at a cottage hospital in an outport. "We needed a break to think about what we wanted to do with our lives," says Mary, who was unhappy and felt as if she had left all of her career opportunities back in the States. "I felt trapped. Here I was with two babies, a morose husband who didn't know what he wanted, and a country in which I was an alien. I yearned for more than the place I had left behind, and perhaps I blamed him too much for my unhappy situation."

After seven months in Newfoundland, Mary's husband accepted a residency position in a Toronto hospital, and they got ready to move again. In their island isolation they had grown less cautious, unaware of increased efforts by U.S. authorities to apprehend draft resisters. While Mary flew to Ohio with the children to visit her family, the doctor drove from the Maritimes, intending to cut through the northeastern states as a shortcut to Toronto. However, at the border his name came up on the computer, and he was immediately jailed on a draft evasion charge in Bangor, Maine, with bail set at $2,500. "That was extremely high," Mary relates. "Even the lawyer was surprised. That was more than some murder suspects were given. I flew to Maine with the kids, we managed to borrow the money from a kind friend in Newfoundland, and we stayed in a cheap motel that the sheriff's relatives owned. We were absolutely broke. Dinner consisted of a take-out special for a buck at the IGA food counter. We took it back to the motel and ate whatever the kids left." Ironically the oppression served to strengthen their marriage. They were united again in a common effort for survival: "We even wondered if unconsciously he had wanted to be caught, to end all these decisions we had to make."

Their local lawyer began negotiating with the army, which finally agreed to take Mary's husband as an enlisted man and drop the charges. Then the air force stepped in and offered him a position as an officer and physician without penalty. Meanwhile Mary got a job at an osteopathic hospital. "I went in for an interview and broke down and cried to the director of nursing. She was very sympathetic and broke some rules in order to get me started immediately. Then a co-worker, whose husband was a sergeant in the air force, found us a trailer in their court. They lent us blankets and gave us food. They were great," Mary recalls.

Next their lawyer informed them that if they were to return to

Canada they would be extradited. Mary contacted a draft resistance group in Montreal, and they explained that this was false information. With this assurance in mind, they began to plan their escape with a group of Quakers that they had met in Bangor. Their time back in the States had taught them not to take anything for granted, so the plans were laid with great care: "We went to a farm on Easter Sunday for sunrise services and met a Quaker minister who offered to help us. We had to use code names if he phoned – his line was tapped. A date was set for us to casually pack the kids into the car and drive north. This was now deadly serious. We couldn't tell anyone what we intended to do. So on a Friday night we began to drive. We had the name of a Quaker family that lived near the border. If we got stopped by the police, we were to say that we were visiting them for the weekend. It was the longest two hours we had ever spent. Every set of headlights that appeared behind us made us sweat. When we got to the border, the French-Canadian guard looked at our papers and waved us through with a smile. You know what we did? We got out of the car and actually kissed the ground! We were home – we were free!"

They settled down again, in Toronto, where they were helped by the Canadian Quakers – the minister from Maine drove all of their belongings up on his own time. But it wasn't over yet. They began to receive more letters, this time from the people who had befriended them in Maine. One letter from a co-worker called them "dirty yellow cowards," and the army sergeant's wife accused them of stealing her blankets. "I did leave the blankets with instructions for them to be returned to her, and I think she eventually got them," Mary says with some sympathy for the woman. "I really think she felt we had betrayed her and that we were traitors. I was hurt and angry again. We were good people who agonized over some very moral and emotional decisions. We didn't deserve such treatment."

In 1977, when most of the 10,000 Vietnam War draft evaders were pardoned, Mary's husband was faced with not only a federal charge of draft evasion, but also a state offence of bail jumping, which was not included in the amnesty. Fearing arrest and imprisonment for up to 10 years, he still couldn't cross the border into the United States. They called the same lawyer in Bangor who had misinformed them about the extradition. For a fee of $500 he had lunch with the district attorney and got the charges dropped. That was the last straw for Mary: "I took out my Canadian citizenship as soon as I could. I was very bitter and anti-American at the time. All we had gone through seemed not to have mattered. Americans thought they could just clear it with an amnesty and welcome us all back. They didn't realize that very few of us wanted to go back. We had somehow survived our hurts and loneliness and made ourselves a new home in a more civilized land."

Mary separated from her husband in 1978, 10 years after following him to Canada. When her children finished high school, she reexamined her decision to live in Canada: "I thought of going back to Ohio to be with my family, but my kids were Canadian and their lives and friends were here. I also realized that I had changed, too. My values were different. I couldn't live in the States anymore."

Mary's children don't share her aversion either to the United States or to the military. Both took advantage of recent changes in American law to acquire dual citizenship status. Her daughter now works as a chemist in Michigan, and her son, who graduated from McGill University with a history degree, has, with an irony not missed by Mary, joined the Canadian naval reserves.

While Mary left her Ohio farm home long ago, its shadowy image emerges in some of her artwork. In one of her pieces – from a series of mixed-media constructions from the eighties – plaster-cast hands appear to be writing on a blackboard reminiscent of a rural school. A hologram of a house combines with the chalkboard phrase, "There's no place like home," creating a dreamlike quality. In her accompanying notes Mary elaborates: "This work is about time, memory, and the idea of 'home' in both a personal and a historical sense. The holographic image creates a depth that allows the chalk words to float within its volume. Home, as memory or dream, remains an illusion for contemporary man."

With her Midwestern American roots long severed, Mary feels that she may be fated for a life of wandering: "I'm very restless again," she says. "Maybe I'll head back east, visit my kids and family again. I also dream of living in Europe and painting there for a while." It is tempting to think of Mary's artwork as a metaphor for this transient impulse. With its eerie, now-you-see-it-now-you-don't images of home set within vibrant sweeps of colour, Mary's work evokes a kind of longing for what has been left behind, while suggesting a desire to set out and discover new terrain.

JOHN CONWAY

Loss and Remembrance

WHILE ATTENDING A conference in Washington, D.C., in the early nineties, John Conway visited the Vietnam War Memorial, an impressive wall of polished black granite that bears the names of more than 58,000 Americans who were killed in the war or who are still listed as missing in action. "I went alone at 6:30 one morning, not looking for a particular name. I wondered in awe at the thousands of names of young people slaughtered due to politics and ambition. It was wrong then and it is wrong now," he says. As with most of the people who came to Canada to avoid taking part in America's war in Vietnam, John stresses that he doesn't fault those who went. He also acknowledges that he was born into the right class and was therefore able to receive an education that enabled him to escape the fate of those who died. But John Conway wasn't born lucky.

His father, a senior executive at the Koehring Crane Company in Milwaukee, died suddenly of ulcers when John was only 12. Like most 12-year-olds, John had much admired his father, who was born in the small Wisconsin town of Edgerton in 1905 and had travelled the world as a young man. He had spent considerable time in Hawaii before returning home to Edgerton and marrying John's mother in 1940 at the age of 35. He promptly got his first regular job as a salesman for the Koehring Crane Company and began his successful climb to the president's office. John, the eldest of two children, was born in 1945. "I led an upper-middle-class, suburban life," he says of the big family home set well away from the working-class world of industrial Milwaukee.

John's mother, in keeping with the times, stayed home while her husband went off to work. Like many others, she suffered massive depression, for which she started receiving electroshock therapy just before her husband's death in 1957. "She had a sad life. She was really manic-depressive most of the years that I can remember. She was hospitalized a lot of the time," recalls John, who also suspects that the shock therapy contributed to her cognitive problems. "When I was in high school and she was home, she often wouldn't get up in the morning or get dressed. She didn't leave the house for years at a time." A widowed aunt on John's mother's side, Rosie, moved in with the fractured family to care for John and his sister. "She was a nurse and a feisty disciplinarian. She was always a strong, no-nonsense kind of person. I was very fond of her after I left home."

John's father hadn't saved a lot of money, but he did leave some investments and, of course, the house. The sale of the latter managed to sustain John's mother until her condition forced her to move into a nursing home. "Then Aunt Rosie died, and because she had saved her money like a squirrel, there was enough for my mother's care until she died."

John had to look outside of his home to form his political philosophy. "I think what shaped me was a certain sensitivity to others. I didn't have it very easy emotionally. I was scared of my mother and, even before he died, my dad was gone a lot. I was left on my own so that I became sensitive and aware of emotional tones in myself and others. I turned into myself a certain amount," he recalls.

Attending a small, publicly supported Catholic boys' high school, John proved himself to be a good student. Run by the Salvatorian Order of priests, the school taught the politics of righteousness. "I shudder when I think of the vice principal. A huge, towering guy who, if you were fooling around too much, would simply punch you out," John recalls wonderingly, realizing that he actually liked the man. But then John didn't fool around. This was his place to try to honour the memory of his father. "I was a good kid. I was involved in all sorts of things. I loved basketball, but couldn't play worth a shit, so I was the manager of the team. I was on the debating team, in the yearbook club. I was even a football cheerleader," he says, laughing.

Success and acceptance at school led John to join the Salvatorian Order in 1963. He attended a small liberal arts college for a year before becoming a novitiate, which involved spending a year at a monastery in the middle of the cornfields of Iowa at Colfax. "There were about 25 of us there. It was a real monastic life. Up with the sun, pray for an hour, and then out to work in the fields. There was no talking during meals and you had to wear all of the garb – I was a very holy guy."

In 1967 John had been in the seminary for four years but had only completed his third year of college. He was beginning to develop a more articulate humanitarian view of the world and had been exposed to the emerging radical wing of the Catholic church, which had drawn its inspiration from the proclamations of Vatican II a few years earlier. The work of the Berrigan brothers, who were from Ohio, influenced John and the other young men of his order. "Father Daniel Berrigan was part of the Milwaukee scene. Many of the priests were influenced by his ideas. Our religious order had vows of poverty, chastity, and obedience, which I took after my year in the monastery. It was a time of tremendous change, and more than half of my peers were leaving the order. There wasn't any pressure to stay, but you were encouraged to consider your options carefully and make an honest decision."

Joining the exodus, John left the order in 1967. He rented an apartment with three other former novitiates and enrolled at Marquette University to complete his bachelor's degree. John continued to participate actively in the church, which was undergoing great change. It was a time when the mass was being translated into English from the traditional Latin, and folk music and guitars were being incorporated into church services. Having shed his religious vows, John met and married, "perhaps too quickly," his first wife, Mary, a fellow student at Marquette. John had been studying philosophy and English at school, but now, in his final year, he began to focus on psychology.

With the pressure of the draft beginning to shape his life, John enrolled in graduate school. Soon after, however, exemptions for "lingering graduate students" were terminated, so John considered seeking conscientious objector status. In 1968 the Milwaukee Fourteen broke into draft board offices and burned files in an effort to make people aware of alternatives to the draft. "I was certain from the very beginning that I was not going to participate in the war. I was going to devote my life to working with people and I had no interest in being a soldier. I was very clear on that," he states emphatically.

With one year of graduate school under his belt, John got a job working with children as a psychology assistant. He believed that working in a health field exempted him from the draft. However, in the summer of 1969 – only three weeks into his job – John was asked to report to his induction centre. "My wife and I had only been married a few months at the time. There was no way that I was going into the reserve or to Vietnam. I didn't really consider going to jail or going underground, either."

The young couple left for Canada within a few days. John's mother was sorry to see her son go, but she was supportive. Mary's parents, who were conservative Ohio Republicans, also understood their decision to leave. When they crossed into Windsor, Ontario, the couple's application for landed immigrant status was aided by the fact that Mary's parents had loaned them $5,000 to carry with them until they reached Toronto, where they would mail it back. With money in their pockets and educations that offered reasonable prospects, they were accepted into Canada after passing a medical exam. They went to Toronto to join a cousin of Mary's who had also recently left the United States. John got a job at the Queen Street Mental Health Centre and began looking for a graduate school where he could continue his education.

He was finally accepted into a master's program at the University of Calgary with a small scholarship. Neither John nor Mary knew anything about Calgary, but that made the move all the more exciting. In classic sixties style they loaded all of their worldly possessions into a Volkswagen microbus and set out across their new country. "Coming into Calgary was a bit of a shock," John recalls. "This prairie town just seemed as if it had parachuted onto the vast landscape."

There were hundreds of Americans from Oklahoma and Texas who were living in Calgary because of the oil industry, but John didn't meet many of these people on the university campus. However, he did get to know a small group of fellow Americans at school who were completely supportive of his actions. These new friends helped the couple to adjust to their new home while John completed his master's degree over the next year. Then, ready to pursue his doctorate in clinical psychology, John and Mary moved to London, where John attended the University of Western Ontario. Mary became the sole income-earner in the couple and began to work as a medical technologist. "There were no draft resisters that I knew of at Western. Except for that first summer in Toronto, I wasn't really hooked into that world. I was just working my butt off in graduate school."

Three years later, with his Ph.D. in hand, John was offered a teaching position at the University of Saskatchewan in Saskatoon. "I didn't really want to go to Saskatchewan, but that's where we wound up in 1973. I've been here ever since. When interest in the social sciences exploded at the end of the sixties, there just weren't enough Canadians to meet the demand. There were four or five other Americans hired at the University of Saskatchewan around the same time."

John went on to set up the Ph.D. program in clinical psychology at the university and to serve as president of the Canadian Psychological Association in 1991. He and Mary have divorced but continue to live close to each other and share in the raising of their son, who is now in university. John married another professor of psychology at the university, and now has a son and a daughter with his new wife. Like many typical middle-class Canadian kids, John's children are enrolled in French immersion but enjoy reading the horror stories of American author R. L. Stine and studying the Korean martial art of tae kwon do.

John's draft evasion story took an ironic twist when, in response to one of the American amnesty offers in the seventies, he contacted an American lawyer to research his case. "The lawyer determined that my file had been open on a desk the night the Milwaukee Fourteen struck. My file was actually burned and they could never have prosecuted me for draft evasion because they didn't have the paperwork," he recounts, obviously enjoying the nonsensical nature of it all.

As he moves into the 50th year of his life, John Conway strikes one as a gentle, mild-mannered academic who is grateful for how good his life in Canada, and at the University of Saskatchewan, has been. He wonders what life would be like if there had been no war in Vietnam and he had stayed in the United States. Would he have found a small, quiet university to teach at, and a peaceful prairie landscape to call his home?

He doesn't have to guess what his life would have been like if he had accepted the draft and gone to Vietnam. When he took his first sabbatical year from the university in 1979, he went to work at a veterans' hospital in Palo Alto, California. "I worked with some Vietnam War vets there," John recalls. "Most of them had spent 10 years or so trying to live a normal family life and more or less just trying to make it. But they had a constant struggle with their war experiences. Some had seen a buddy's head blown off, some had killed civilians. They would experience uncontrollable rage, nightmares, and flashbacks. Their marriages and jobs fell apart as a result of this struggle."

As he listened to them recount what had happened in Vietnam and after, John felt a crushing sadness at the amount of pain that clearly persists so long after the war's end. No matter what their stories, he empathizes with them. He is neither critical of them for having gone to war, nor of himself for having escaped it. The fact remains that, for a generation of young Americans in the sixties, the power struggles and political games of a few old men had an irrevocable impact on their lives. The tens of thousands whose names are etched on the wall in Washington, the millions who are haunted by memories of Vietnam, and the many who found refuge in Canada are all connected by their experiences of the war. John's visit to the Vietnam War Memorial, with its lengthy, and disturbing, list of the dead, and his troubling encounters with those who lived, have proven him to be an integral part of that connection.

MICHAEL BOUGHN

Orange Juice Kid

THE ORANGE JUICE KIDS – that's how the children of Southern California looked to a Canadian boy like myself watching the movies of the fifties and sixties. They all lived in a beautiful, sun-drenched land in big houses with big kitchens in which doting mothers and understanding fathers smiled benevolently as they handed them giant glasses of freshly squeezed orange juice. These kids were always rushing out to jump in the "woody" and go surfing with girls like the innocent, yet slightly exotic-looking, Annette Funicello.

A charter member of that generation, Michael Boughn grew up in Riverside, California, the grandson of an executive at Sunkist, one of the companies that made those big glasses of orange juice. Born in the spring of 1946, as his father returned to civilian life from the American military's triumphant occupation of Japan, Michael found his child-hood filled with all the symbols of plenitude of the post-Depression era. The family's big ranch house, overlooking the Santa Ana River, was designed and decorated to perfection by a stay-at-home mother who was a Frank Lloyd Wright and Ayn Rand fan. But Michael's youth was also cursed with many of the hidden deceits of the time: "Growing up in Southern California had this advantage: it prepared you for the late 20th century by giving you no culture, no history, and by not covering that absence over with rebuilt gas lamps and stories about George Washington having slept down the street. The closest we got to that kind of illusion of historical continuity and meaning was the art deco statue of Juan Bautista de Anza in the little park downtown. As a kid, when I asked my mother who he was, she told me, repeating her own father's racist historiography, that he was just some horse thief. Ah, America."

Michael's quality of life was also compromised by family problems – the main one stemming from alcohol, the culturally acceptable drug of the era. "My mother's father and brothers were alcoholics and so was she. On my paternal side, only the brother of my father's adoptive mother was an alcoholic, but my father became one all the same. I think for my parents, as kids who survived the Depression and came of age during the war, there was a lot of drinking at that time. Then, by the fifties, it was party time, and nobody seemed to think that there was any danger in it. My mother lived by her father's motto that 'If you're going to drink coffee, drink it black. If you're going to drink whiskey, drink it straight.' There was this whole macho romance tied in with it. Certainly growing up in this kind of environment paved the way for my own self-destructive use of drugs over several years. I was lucky to survive. I knew a lot of people who didn't."

But Michael was at least fortunate enough to be able to take advantage of the well-funded public school system of the fifties and sixties. "I was really scrawny, so I was never very much into sports," he says, "but I really enjoyed the academic side of school. I wrote poetry for the high school literary magazine and hung out with my group of friends. We were considered the nerds, but we were also a little wild. In 1963, when I was 17 years old, we started to develop a political consciousness when a friend hitchhiked to San Bernardino to buy a copy of Jack Kerouac's *On the Road*. It made the rounds and everybody became actively anti-establishment. We called ourselves the Committee of Eleven and we put out an illegal newsletter that mocked the student government. If it hadn't been for my choir teacher, I would have been kicked out of school."

Michael's parents, especially his father, were quite dismayed by his emerging, somewhat radical, values. His original plans to become a lawyer or an FBI agent, like his father's friend, were quickly fading. The images of racial oppression in Selma and Little Rock were searing themselves into the American consciousness and, in 1963, he joined the American Civil Liberties Union. "It was a time when I was really caught up in the revolutionary romance of Jeffersonian American democracy. I was reading Howard Fast's book on Tom Paine called *Common Sense*."

After graduating from high school in 1964, Michael enrolled at the University of California. But, at the end of his first year, he decided to go to Europe. He arranged a ride to New York and bought a ticket on a freighter to Tangier. In dropping out of university, however, Michael became eligible for the draft. The day before he was to leave he received his draft notice in the mail, informing him to report for his physical in four months. Believing that America's power was everywhere and that he would be stopped crossing the border into Europe, he cancelled his original plans and went to Mexico with some friends instead. On a small island in the bay at Mazatlán they put the threat of war behind them and worked and drank with the fishermen.

While in Mexico two of Michael's friends got severe bowel infections that gained both of them medical exemptions from the draft. Michael returned to California and enrolled in university for the spring semester of 1966 in order to reobtain his student deferment. But Vietnam was heating up, and he was told that he could only defer for one semester. He received another notice to report for the draft in the summer of 1966: "I freaked out and drove to New York with some friends. We went to a huge old building that was a warren of left-wing organizations, and I got a job there working in a draft counselling organization. Up until then I had thought someone would come along and tell me that everything would be okay, but I now knew that I had no choice but to go to Canada."

Like so many others before and after him, Michael had looked at the conscientious objector option and rejected it. "My father told me that it would kill my grandmother if I did that, and her life would be on my head. The culture that he was part of was completely uncritical of war. They still thought all wars were World War II, which was 'the good war.' Now it was my generation's turn to uphold freedom. They couldn't bear the social shame that would go along with their son publicly announcing such a position. Still, I refused conscientious objector status because I wanted to go to Canada, not because they were putting pressure on me to do so."

By the time he returned from New York to attend his physical, he had devised a plan: "I decided that I would try to get out of being drafted by taking LSD. Plus I didn't shower for days. What a trip that was! It turned into a Tolkienesque fantasy. The acid was peaking and I was going totally out of my mind. The horrible thing was that they were going to draft me, anyway. They knew I was stoned, but they believed that all I needed was a little discipline and a shower, and then they would turn me into a killing machine. It was 90 degrees in Los Angeles and this army sergeant was tormenting me, so I freaked out, leaped up, and grabbed him. Then they threw me out onto the street. A friend picked me up and I spent the night at his house."

When Michael went home, his mother gave him an ultimatum: "Straighten up and join the army, or get out of the house." He packed his bags and left. It was 1966, and all he knew about Canada was what he had learned from an article that he had read in the *San Francisco Chronicle*. He and his friend David hitchhiked to Berkeley and then to Reed College in Portland, Oregon, where they watched the Los Angeles Dodgers play in the World Series. After this final, classic American indulgence, their friends drove them to the border. "When we got there, they split us up. The guy David got was pretty reactionary and hostile. Fortunately the guy I spoke to was very paternal and very nice and was also probably antiwar. I told him that we wanted to homestead in Quebec. He said we should go to the Peace River Valley if we wanted to homestead, and then he approved us for immigration. We ended up going to Vancouver, where we found ourselves amid a group of extremely generous and supportive people – mostly academics – who got us settled in a house with other draft resisters."

Michael found some striking, and at the same time pleasing, differences about Canada: "I remember seeing some New Democratic Party campaign signs and being knocked out by the progressive idea of a socialist party. A third party! I also just couldn't get over how many trees there were, and how much water. Coming from the desert, it was just astonishing."

After spending the winter in a house full of hippies in the west side Vancouver neighbourhood of Kitsilano, Michael got a job planting trees out in the Squamish area of British Columbia with the B.C. Forest Service. "I felt so damn Canadian doing that. I was up in the bush living in a logging camp near these huge glacial rivers. I had never seen so much water." Earning enough money to travel, Michael set out for Montreal to attend Expo 67. "Somebody had a Volkswagen that was running on three cylinders. We just jumped in and drove out east. We met a whole bunch of other hippies in Montreal. It was the summer of love in San Francisco and that culture was everywhere. It was all so wonderfully exotic."

But things went horribly wrong for Michael in Montreal. "In spite of all the adventure, things were pretty bleak for me in those days. I was painfully alienated from my family, deeply lonely, and screwed up in ways that I wouldn't become aware of for years. In that context I took some acid with some friends and almost killed myself. The whole world just turned to shit in front of my eyes. I began to hear angelic voices and I started to climb a tree to chase them, and I literally went off the top of the tree. When they scraped me off the ground, I was clutching the top of the tree in my hand. I had shattered my neck."

Michael was taken to a hospital in Montreal. Contrary to his wishes, the hospital contacted his parents and his father arrived immediately. "He showed up, stayed two days, complained about the heat, and left. I'm still angry about this even though he's been dead for years. To give him his due, his alcoholism was very advanced. He was in massive denial about everything. He was fundamentally a good man, but he wasn't the kind of man who could take control. He really wanted us to be like the family on the TV show *Father Knows Best*, but he didn't quite know how."

While most Canadians welcomed the young men who fled the United States to avoid serving in the Vietnam War, there were those who resented their presence here. One such individual, a right-wing radio talk show host, took an interest in Michael's case while he was still in the hospital. On his show Michael was presented as an irresponsible, drug-taking draft evader whose hospital stay was costing the Canadian taxpayer a lot of money. Needless to say, the entire experience was a particularly unsettling one for Michael and, after his recovery, he decided to return to the West Coast and go back to school.

It was the fall of 1967 – he had been in Canada for one very hectic year – and he went to live in a cooperative house in New Westminster, just outside of Greater Vancouver. The others in the house were all Simon Fraser University students, and Michael began to hang out on campus and enrolled in a course on the works of Charles Olson offered by the poet Robin Blaser. "Robin's example, as poet and thinker, changed my life. Although I later quarrelled with him over politics, and was then estranged from him during my years as a political activist in the labour movement, I never lost my admiration for him and his work. Eventually I was able to reestablish a relationship with him. In fact, a couple of years ago I organized a reading for him in Buffalo and, just this year [1995], I was fortunate enough to be able to read a paper in honour of him at his 70th birthday celebration in Vancouver."

During 1968 and 1969, political consciousness was on the rise at Simon Fraser University and demonstrations at the school resembled many of those taking place on other campuses throughout North America. Students were organizing sit-ins at the administration building in order to fight for increased participation in governing the school. Michael completed five consecutive semesters at Simon Fraser during those two years. However, in the fall of 1969 he decided to drop out of school once again. Undergoing a brief period of transiency, Michael returned to Montreal that year, only to move back to Vancouver in the spring of 1970.

In that summer of 1970 the Hudson's Bay Company hosed down hippies who were holding a sit-in in front of their downtown store. At a subsequent demonstration, in which Michael participated, the American flag was burnt in front of the U.S. consulate. As the crowd of protesters marched up Granville Street following the ceremony, the police mistook a spectator for a flag-burner and arrested him, leaving his distraught girlfriend behind. Michael and his friend Richard volunteered to go down to the police station with her to help get her boyfriend out of jail. "While we were inside the cop shop an angry crowd surrounded the station. One of the brass came up to me and Richard and told us that we had to go out and calm the crowd." Asking for a bullhorn, Michael and Richard went out and stood on the front steps of the police station. Richard raised the bullhorn to his mouth and, at full volume, yelled, "There's only five of them inside. Charge!" He then leaped into the crowd with Michael right behind him, and they made their escape. At the same time the riot squad arrived and dispersed the mob.

Inspired by the energy of the many antiwar protests spreading across North America, students from the political science department of Simon Fraser University formed the Vancouver Liberation Front (VLF). Michael and Richard joined the organization, and thus began a long and intense journey through the many radical, and often highly competitive, movements of the period. Michael defines his group affiliation with a pragmatic élan garnered from years of attendance at meetings and a slice of mature cynicism that only slightly moderates his commitment to the ideals of the era. "In the VLF people were trying to formalize the political energy of the time to promote agitation in the city around issues of poverty and imperialism. The same kind of thing was happening all over the world. There were the Black Panthers in the United States and the Cultural Revolution in China, which at that time seemed like a very progressive thing, not to mention the FLQ in Canada. We did a lot to help people on welfare. We also occupied Stanley Park once for three or four days in an attempt to liberate the whales. Phil Ochs came up from the United States and sang for our cause. Most of the guys who were leading the group were Marxists. They were 25 years old and they wanted a revolution, and to be in control – now! Then there were people like Richard and me, who had been reading the Romantic poets. Our revolutionary attitude was more of a visionary, Blakean kind of thing. In fact, the VLF operated out of five or six collective houses – ours was called Blake House."

The youthful enthusiasm and idealism of the sixties, fuelled by a very real anger at the hypocrisy of previous generations, was creating some interesting political alliances. Many of the leaders of the youth-inspired groups used this exciting birth of consciousness to try to obtain long-term commitments from their members: "In about 1972 we made contact with the Marxist-Leninist division of the Communist Party in Canada, which had begun as the Internationalists in 1962. Their leadership shipped us all off to Toronto. My take on it now is that it was a cult. One of the things that a cult will do in order to maintain control is to place you in unfamiliar situations and then break up all of your relationships so that you no longer have any links to your old life. What they wanted us to believe was that we were involved in a serious party that was seriously planning a revolution."

At the time Michael was seeing a woman who was originally from Scotland – with whom he later had a daughter – and they were both assigned to the same group in Toronto by the party leadership. The control of the young workers was oppressive and mean-spirited. Michael has since based some of his writing on the experience; particularly one of his short stories, "Headache," based on his experience of working on the party newspaper while suffering from a severe head cold. Harassment was an effective way to keep the guilt and anger of the members focused on the party needs. "I was deeply angry," Michael recalls. "As I get older, I can see that a lot of that anger came from my own family history. I was enraged at my parents but, on the other hand, I don't want to underestimate the political rage that I was experiencing, too. We were turning on the TV every night and watching the napalming of women and children. It was a nightmare that we felt had to be stopped."

Michael was involved with the Communist Party in Canada for almost seven years. He finally broke all ties to the organization in 1978. Of those seven intense years he is philosophical: "It's curious the way the best of intentions can lead you into the worst of situations. So many of the people involved in the party were motivated by a selfless devotion to the idea of justice – to the desire to see a reign of justice in the world – only to find themselves trapped in a cult where they were manipulated to satisfy the whims of a power-hungry elite. It's the same old story. Still, better, as they say, to have loved and lost. And at the very least we helped keep that dream of justice alive."

At about the same time that he quit the party his relationship with the woman from Scotland ended, and their young daughter went to live with her mother. Charges laid against him in the United

States for draft evasion were quietly dropped in 1976, so Michael went to visit his parents in California for the first time in 12 years. Back in his old hometown he began to feel "that there was a me that had never been allowed to come into being. I had totally repressed the part of myself that wanted to go back or wanted to know what life might have been like if I hadn't had to leave the United States. You can't afford to ask those kinds of questions when you can't do anything about them. Suddenly the questions started to come up." Michael returned to Toronto, packed his 1969 Chevy Nova, and drove back to California where he got work at a metal stamping factory in the Silicon Valley: "I ended up running a punch press for two and a half years."

In 1980 he visited Vancouver again and met with Robin Blaser, who inspired his return to school at the University of California in Santa Cruz. It took him another two years to complete his bachelor of arts degree in English: "At first I was working and going to school at the same time, reading Homer in the warehouse. But then I decided to take out a student loan and just do it full-time." On the recommendation of one of his professors, Michael enrolled in graduate school at the State University of New York in Buffalo where Robert Creeley taught. "I thought about studying under one of my favourite authors and being nearer to my daughter in Toronto, and that pretty much confirmed my decision to go."

Michael graduated with a Ph.D. in 1989 and began doing book design and publishing. He also taught writing part-time and was prepared to settle in Buffalo for life. "I didn't want to return to the uptight Anglo enclave of Toronto, but then I met Liz when I was visiting my daughter and I fell in love." He tried to commute between the two cities but, a year after marrying Liz, he finally left Buffalo and moved back to Toronto for good. He has come to understand his anger with his parents and the society that shaped them, and looks back upon his life with a mix of amazement that he has survived and with pride in his accomplishments. There is pride, too, in his grown child.

Today Michael lives within walking distance of the University of Toronto where he teaches English to a generation of students whose only sense of the sixties has been gleaned from history books. He continues to publish his own poetry and fiction, as well as the works of others, through his Shuffaloff Press. Life on the tree-lined streets and in the coffee shops and restaurants along Bloor Street West in Toronto is good, and although he may have mellowed somewhat, he has done so without surrendering any of his social commitment.

But still, reflecting on the years of his youth, he laments, "It's with a kind of sadness that I look back now. A sadness for what we all had to give up because of the greed, arrogance, and stupidity of those who insisted on pursuing that war even after they knew it was wrong. I mean all of us, veterans and resisters alike. We were all victims of the arrogance of power that Robert McNamara has finally admitted to. Who knows what kind of world we could have built had all that energy been turned to creation rather than to war and destruction."

JAMES LESLIE

Flight from Privilege

IN THE FIFTIES the United States was considered a fairly privileged place to grow up. While most of the world was healing from the wounds left by World War II, American kids were going to movies that told of their country's heroic soldiers who had risked their lives to defend peace and liberty. The concepts of freedom and the free world took on mythic proportions. These were ideas that American children committed themselves to each morning in school with the Pledge of Allegiance. But while every child took the pledge, not every child was considered equal under the American educational system. Southern blacks were forced to attend poorly funded, segregated schools, and thousands of Native American children were taken hundreds of miles away from their homes to attend residential schools designed to "cleanse them" of their traditional culture.

For the majority of the emerging middle class, though, fine new schools were being built in the suburban housing developments that mushroomed around the cities in that era. Like the houses in which their students lived, these new schools were marvels of interior design, with favourable lighting, modern furnishings, high-tech audiovisual equipment, and well-stocked libraries. But there was also a third level of schooling, available to the old, and new, corporate elite. Located mostly in the northeastern United States, a series of fine institutions, somewhat in the tradition of the British public school, served the children of the nation's political and financial leaders.

Highly ranked among these, Phillips Exeter Academy is set in the New Hampshire countryside, 50 miles north of Boston. The graduates of this boarding school typically go on to study at Yale, Harvard, or Princeton. If they attend university in California, they usually enroll at Stanford rather than at Berkeley. It has been the prep school of choice for the children of many of America's power brokers since its founding in 1781. Daniel Webster was the first of many famous alumni. More recent graduates include Gore Vidal and John Irving, one of whose books is based on the school. The school's establishment clientele can expect an intellectually stimulating atmosphere, with an impressive library and intimate, roundtable-style classes. In the ultraconservative fifties, Phillips Exeter Academy was often viewed as the most liberal and progressive of its type.

When James Leslie's family enrolled him at the academy in the mid-fifties, it wasn't so much to shape him in the conservative mould of the time, as to follow the prescribed way of life for upper-middle-class American youth. "My dad was a semiprogressive Republican – what you would call a Red Tory in Canada today," says 54-year-old health services planner Leslie, sitting on the top floor of the refurbished craftsman-style house to which he and his family have recently moved. The windows of his home look out over the rooftops of the neighbourhood of Kitsilano, located on Vancouver's west side which,

25 years ago, was considered a hippie area.

But James makes it abundantly clear that his father was "not of the manor born." Rather, as a young man he had run away to sea and been "busted" from the U.S. Coast Guard. James's uncles had established themselves in finance in New York City in the twenties and brought his father into their business. He subsequently took some training in the field and displayed a natural aptitude for the business which, in turn, led to a successful career in finance. But James never saw his father as a perfect fit with the upper-middle-class lifestyle that they led. Unlike many of his associates, he hadn't attended a school like Phillips Exeter or achieved a formal university education.

Like many families in the fifties, the Leslies didn't spend a lot of time together and the children led fairly sheltered lives in their removed boarding school worlds: "Exeter presented a view of America as a meritocracy," says James. "The structures were there that would equalize opportunity so that those who wanted to struggle and work hard could find their way into positions of leadership if they were virtuous and intelligent. It was the best part of the American myth that was fed to us. Because it was such a nice elitist place, you didn't get too many insights into the true corruptions of the country."

Not a lot changed when James graduated from Phillips Exeter in the class of 1959 and then went on to do his undergraduate degree in history at Stanford University. "It was standard for upper-middle-class kids to go directly on to college and to avoid the draft," explains James. "You just planned to go straight on through to graduate school until you were 26 years old and no longer eligible to serve."

James did a lot of partying in his first years at Stanford, but he also joined a group of students who were taking over a fraternity and attempting to alter its agenda: "We wanted to create a place where intelligent people could get together. A place that valued diversity." By eliminating the hazing rituals and removing the racial exclusion clause from the charter, the fraternity was suspended from national membership. Over the next decade it grew into a co-ed gathering place where students and faculty mingled and shared ideas. James still feels good about his part in this early questioning of American establishment values that had shaped so much of the fifties through larger institutions such as the House Un-American Activities Committee. At the same time he doesn't consider the fraternity protest to have been a real turning point in his own political development. He wasn't one of the fraternity's budding politicians, many of whom were involved in a sort of liberal anticommunism: "They went off to these international youth conferences to counter the Communists. At the same time they carried on with the liberal program against the populist hysteria of McCarthyism."

In his final year at Stanford James, who had achieved a reputation as a somewhat "notorious drunk," was suspended from the school for the second semester. He took his tuition rebate, bought a little Vespa scooter, loaded his possessions on it, and drove to San Francisco. He then crossed the Bay and went to the marshalling yards of the Southern Pacific Railway in Oakland, where he got a job as a switchman. A new kind of education began for James. It was during the time that the railways were moving out of the passenger business and jobs were opening up in the previously all-white switching yards for displaced black porters. Many of the white workers felt that their jobs were threatened by the incoming blacks and there was a constant danger of deliberately caused "accidents." As an outsider to both the white blue-collar worker and the black man, James was able to learn from and, to some extent, be accepted by both groups. "I found that I really enjoyed the company of the people that I was working with," he recalls. "I was learning about racial politics and technology-driven shifts in the economy that moved black workers into new areas of work."

While in Oakland James attended a few lectures at Berkeley and was exposed to some of the power of the growing Free Speech Movement. In September 1964 he went back to finish his bachelor of arts degree at Stanford. Uncertain about his graduate school opportunities or interests, he registered in the reserves as a cook in order to avoid the draft. Because the Vietnam War had not yet taken centre stage in the American consciousness, this wasn't considered an unusual thing to do. Avoiding the draft just meant getting out of three years of drudgery; it was no more a moral choice than taking advantage of a tax deduction. "I thought it was a time of peace. It looked like the Johnsons of the world had triumphed over the Goldwater types and the cold war and the military effort were on their way out. So one could go into the reserves as a cook – a neutral, nonviolent job – as one way of dealing with the military."

The reserves required six months of active duty, participation in a summer camp, joining a unit, and going to meetings once in a while. A person on the move could arrange to get out of all but the six months of active duty. Similar to his experience working as a switchman, James's time in the reserves served to further enlighten him about facets of American society that he had never known at Phillips Exeter or at Stanford. Posted in Monterey, he recalls that, "In part, it was just tedious and awful, but another part of it gave me new insight into life in America – insight that I found horrific. It was about moving into a structure of complete control. Until then I enjoyed freedom of choice. If I wanted to be an angst-ridden young man in university, I could."

In the military James was subjected to a kind of control previously unknown to him: "If I had told some officer to go fuck himself, I would have gone to prison. That was a constraint that I hadn't experienced before." He was most disturbed, however, by the loss of selfhood necessitated by military service: "The real horror was the uniformity and mindlessness of it all. It was a land of totally stultifying greyness. Nothing could stand out – from the buildings, to the uniforms, to the ashen colour that we all became."

James also learned that people's lives were expendable in the military. When an outbreak of spinal meningitis hit the camp, he saw soldiers refused for sick call and ordered back to their units. They later passed out on the parade ground and then died. Things just carried on as usual while the death toll grew. By the time some action to prevent the further spread of the disease was taken, James had started to apply some of his analytical skills to the situation: "I learned that it was endemic. You always have a higher incidence of meningitis in military locations because people from a lot of different places are brought together under crowded conditions. While examining the situation I also began to look at the number of men who came in with pulmonary disease, and I learned that there were as many people dying from pneumonia as from meningitis. The lives of men drafted into the military simply didn't have much value."

James completed his basic training in October 1964. He had already been exposed to the Free Speech Movement erupting at Berkeley and he had heard about the growth of the Civil Rights Movement in the South from a friend in the reserves. He now wanted to learn more about both. While Americans were being told that their country would maintain a limited involvement in Vietnam, James was informed that the real agenda was to place 50,000 troops there by the end of the year. On August 7, 1964, the U.S. Congress had passed the Gulf of Tonkin Resolution, giving President Johnson extraordinary power to act in Southeast Asia. Later that month American warplanes had bombed North Vietnam.

James left for Berkeley in late 1964 to act on his growing political consciousness and to become more involved in the antiwar movement. He traces the birth of the peace movement on the West Coast to events that took place earlier that year. A number of demonstrations and civil disobedience actions were carried out by the Free Speech Movement in 1964 while James was still in the military. The protests culminated with the occupation of Sproul Plaza at Berkeley by 1,000 students. In a speech to the group of student demonstrators, their leader, Mario Savio, linked their struggle for free political expression to the national fight for civil rights: "Last summer I went to Mississippi to join the struggle there for civil rights. This fall I am engaged in another phase of the same struggle, this time in Berkeley. The two battlefields may seem quite different to some observers, but this is not the case. The same rights are at stake in both places – the right to participate as citizens in a democratic society and the right to due process of law."

Although the students were eventually evicted by a force of 600 police officers, the university's academic senate granted the demonstrators' demands for free political activity on campus. This victory was particularly important for people who, like James, were now testing the concept of freedom in the United States. In the meantime the Civil Rights Movement, which had attracted many young liberal whites to the cause, was beginning to move under the command of black organizations. Consequently young white activists of the New Left began to focus on an issue that would bear directly on themselves – the Vietnam draft.

On April 17, 1965, the Students for a Democratic Society rallied 20,000 people and marched on Washington. But within three months there were 18 American combat battalions in Vietnam and, on July 28, 1965, Johnson approved General Westmoreland's request for another 44 combat battalions. In California the students at Berkeley realized that many of these troops were being embarked at the nearby Oakland Army Terminal. So, in August of that same year, the Oakland branch of the Students for a Democratic Society and the Vietnam Day Committee organized a sit-in on the railway tracks at a point where the trains had to pass through Berkeley. James was among the 300 or so people on the tracks: "It was quite incredible. The troop train came along with a phalanx of police officers ahead of it. They just threw everybody off the track. I remember being stunned by the raw force that was used. I stood on a bank by the tracks, looking at the soldiers in the Pullman cars, and sensed how far away we really were from them. I was feeling how much more power they had – not as individuals, but as parts of something larger. I realized then that this was the big leagues."

At about the same time as the Oakland demonstration James's family moved to Santa Monica, where his father became the senior financial manager for the Douglas Aircraft Corporation. He and his mother went to the opening of a park in the Santa Monica mountains to which Douglas had contributed some funds. When it was time to leave, they caught a ride on one of the company's helicopters and James was forced to face a huge contradiction in his life: "We came gliding down out of the mountains and landed in the middle of Douglas Aircraft's main plant. There I was, a Marxist-Leninist opposed to the war in Vietnam, landing in the middle of the assembly area for Atlas missiles. There was a nuclear holocaust sitting right there at my father's office, the finance guru of Douglas Aircraft, and his Communist son was driving right through it. The juxtaposition was just overwhelming."

James then became involved with a group that sought to organize reservists against the war. But the danger of treason charges, coupled with the fact that the organization's offices were being bombed, served to cool much of the group's enthusiasm. "We just didn't have the tenacity to go very far," he recalls. "Nothing was ever done about the bombings, and the larger organizations weren't too eager to support us. College-kid demonstrations were one thing, but going up against the military was quite another."

James also points out that he and his friends didn't have a very clear understanding of the CIA and FBI substructures. "We knew that they were around, but we didn't want to become paranoid. People were operationally naive at the time. Being spied upon by our government wasn't something that we were thinking about. I later realized that because I was the son of a Douglas Aircraft executive, and was also involved with leftist groups, I was probably being watched."

James was accepted at the Hastings College of Law at the University of California in the fall of 1965. He completed his first semester but didn't continue. "I wanted to be a progressive, lefty lawyer, but then, after the Watts riots in Los Angeles, I came to understand that the goddamn law didn't protect anybody – the system had collapsed. It was also at that time that political activism seemed to hit the wall. Everybody started getting into drugs, and the centre of activity moved from Berkeley over to San Francisco," he explains. "The pervasive feeling at the time was that 'politics sucked,' and the world needed to be re-created. That was the origin of Haight-Ashbury. There was a lot of anticommunism inherent in that stance. People were opposed to ideology. They were turning to the communes, drugs, and sex to find something deeper."

After dropping out of Hastings, James enrolled at San Francisco State University to obtain a teaching credential. The program was dynamically linked to city life, and James became involved in a project called "Upward Bound," which brought kids from a wide range of ethnic backgrounds together to attend school on the university campus. These were students who weren't functioning well in the normal educational system, but who were perceived to have scholastic potential. The results of the program were incredibly rewarding: "A lot of those kids got really involved. A number them even joined the Black Panthers. Some went on to city and state colleges, and others to universities across the state."

This experience moved James to the point that he felt he had finally found his place in the world, but he still hadn't dealt with his military commitment and the expectations of his reserve unit. They finally ordered him to report to camp. He sent the orders back with a covering letter telling his superiors that he felt he was many things – a Buddhist, a Christian, and a Jew – but he wasn't a soldier, and he challenged the legitimacy of their authority. James was thus faced with three options: to go to jail, to go underground, or to leave the country. "I wasn't going to let them send me to jail and life underground seemed preposterous – it meant allowing them to make your life into that of a desperado's."

Just before Christmas of 1967 James went to Canada, applied for landed immigrant status, and was accepted. He headed to Vancouver and got in touch with Mac Elrod, a Baptist minister and a university librarian, through a war resisters' group. After staying with Mac for a little while, he travelled up the Sunshine Coast and found work as a substitute teacher. However, upon discovering that he wasn't getting called to work because the teachers at the secondary school considered him a "Communist coward," he returned to the city and got involved with an alternative school. "I just didn't feel rooted, though. It was a profoundly difficult experience being cut off from everything I had known."

So, in the summer of 1968, James travelled across Canada and settled in Montreal, where he found work as a teacher in a private college preparation program. He soon connected with a deserters' group there, the American Friends Service Committee, which took a clearly political stance on the war in Vietnam and was trying to encourage more draft evaders to move to Canada. They were also lobbying the Canadian government not to have deserter status count against Americans in the immigration process. It was a relatively small group and, because he could speak a bit of French, James became their spokesperson. At the same time he felt compelled to start developing a Canadian identity: "I began to feel the need to start focusing on Canadian issues rather than on American ones. I wanted to become aware of Canadian history and Canadian politics." After a couple of years, James moved to Toronto. He had fallen in love with a Canadian woman there, whom he eventually married. That move marked the end of James's active participation in the antiwar movement.

James was absorbed by his work as an outreach worker for the YMCA and a settlement house when President Carter offered amnesty to most of the Vietnam War draft evaders in 1977. He returned to the United States, underwent a low-level court-martial, and received an unsuitable-for-service discharge. He was a bit concerned that his earlier antiwar activities would cause some problems, but through the American Friends Service Committee and the Freedom of Information Act, his military record was reviewed ahead of time and the process was completed without any delay.

Returning to Canada, James immersed himself in his community work, which he continues to do today. The work now involves
health services consulting, much of it for First Nations communities
that want to take charge of their health-care programs. Such work
stems directly from those earlier days working with street kids in San
Francisco, but the social commitment is rooted more deeply in the
progressive liberal education he received at Phillips Exeter and in the
American universities he attended in the fifties and sixties.

Looking back on those early years, James notes how removed it
all seems from his present life, yet recognizes how it has all shaped
his identity: "I was raised in a fairly liberal society by a father who
believed in the underlying beneficence of the state. I learned that a
thinking individual is a moral individual. When faced with participation in the military, I deemed the reserves to be morally neutral,
but the advent of American involvement in Vietnam changed the
equation, and I came to Canada. When I crossed the border, it was
irrevocable. I couldn't go back." And James Leslie wouldn't want to.

JOHN THOMPSON

From Penury to Plenitude

"BECAUSE I CAME to Canada mainly for economic reasons, I'm not really sure that I'm a bona fide draft evader," John Thompson wrote in response to my search for people who came to Canada in order to avoid taking part in the Vietnam War. An economic refugee from the United States to Canada? My interest was aroused. A month later I met with John in his pleasant apartment on the third floor of a red-brick house in Toronto, near Bloor Street West, and he filled me in on the details of his story.

"I was never called to report for the draft. I simply became delinquent," says John, who also suggests that even that decision wasn't particularly deliberate. In 1968, 15 months after his arrival in Canada, John received a phone call from the Royal Canadian Mounted

Police. "You know why we're calling, don't you?" the pleasant officer inquired. In fact, John didn't know, but he reported to the police as he was asked. "We discussed everything. The officers were actually two very nice guys and, in the end, we shook hands and they wished me good luck. The following year I was contacted again, but they said they were looking for someone else. Still, I think that was just a pretext to question me and see what I was doing."

These incidents alerted John that the American authorities were on the lookout for him. Consequently he avoided crossing the border into the United States, even though he had had rheumatic fever as a child and believed that he might have qualified for a medical exemption: "I didn't need the hassle, so I just didn't bother going into the States. My brother is five years younger than I am and he had registered for the draft at the consulate. He was subject to the lottery, but he was never called."

Born and raised in Ironton, in the extreme south of Ohio, John says simply, "I have no good memories of that place." When I prompt him on reminiscences of teenage years there, he adds, ". . . except for school." With that, he unfolds a tale of loneliness and isolation in a small, unfriendly town. His mother, an upper-middle-class Belgian woman, had come to the United States as the war bride of a working-class man from Appalachia. His family had lived in the Kentucky hills for years before moving to Ashland in the northeastern part of the state. They then uprooted themselves and moved again, this time across the Ohio River to Ironton.

By the fifties, the town of Ironton and its surrounding area, which had supplied much of the iron for the Civil War, had become a depressed backwater. The population of 16,000 in 1950 showed a steady decline to 15,000 by 1960. John's father was one of those who left. Life was hard, and with the added difficulty of a cross-cultural marriage in a town that was grossly intolerant of differences, John's father could no longer bear the pressure. The alluring young American GI that the Belgian girl once knew was now a frustrated and disgruntled veteran who deserted his family when John was about 12 years old.

John knows where his father is living now, but he doesn't have any contact with him. "I don't hold it against his relatives, though. I've met his brother-in-law only once, but I am in touch with him quite regularly. I've met my father's older brother, too."

Life got tougher. John helped pay for his Catholic schooling with money from his paper route. His mother was forced to accept welfare benefits, but these were very limited. Times were tough. John explains, "Twenty percent of the county was receiving government surplus food, which consisted of rancid flour, rice that had weevils in it, cheese with a thick crust that had to be cut off, powdered eggs, ground-up beef parts, and peanut butter so thick it stuck to the roof of your mouth. There were those who would complain about 'all the fat people coming in taxis to get their surplus food.' They didn't realize that we had no car to take the food away in, and that people were fat not because they were overeating, but because they were eating the wrong things."

There were, however, some small shelters from this bitterly difficult life, even in Ironton. "That town had a very good public library," John recalls. "The Briggs Library was part of a tradition of philanthropy, and I suppose my brother and I were the beneficiaries of that, because we were in the library all the time." Not surprisingly then, by the time he was in senior high school, John was reading Sartre, Nietzsche, Hegel, Kant, Bertrand Russell, and other European philosophers. "It was really existential stuff," he says, explaining that he isn't familiar with Jack Kerouac and other beat writers. John says that he was also beginning to enjoy chemistry at this time, and it was the expectation that he could find a career in this field that motivated him to work hard at school throughout his teenage years.

Many people who grew up in the United States during the fifties and sixties have fond memories of driving around in their parents' cars and, later, in "wheels" of their own. No doubt there were many teenagers cruising the streets of Ironton in the two-tone showboats of the late fifties, but they weren't part of John's world. "My mom had an old 1953 Buick parked outside. One day the police came upstairs to where we lived in an old house and said, 'Your car has been out in the same spot for over a week and that's a parking violation.' Little did they know that it had been parked in the same place for two years! There were weeds from the pavement growing up inside the car. We pushed it into a garage and then someone gave us $50 for it. That was the last we saw of that car."

In spite of having grown up in an isolated corner of the world, John was nevertheless exposed to a broader range of political ideas than many American children in more cosmopolitan centres. "One of the reasons that I'm very happy to be living in Canada is because of the privilege to vote socialist. I was already a socialist by the fifth or sixth grade," John claims with some pride. When asked how he became a socialist in Ironton, Ohio, in the fifties, John replies with a smile, "My mother was getting European magazines from Belgium and she told me about these things. If you knew anything about Europe, you knew about socialism."

Although John's mother was able to get occasional, small jobs, it became clear that there was really no place for a foreign-born single parent in this small Midwestern town. Then, just as John was graduating from high school in 1966, a little money from an inheritance arrived. With a few additional funds raised by borrowing against the family furniture, they abandoned most of their possessions and boarded the Chesapeake & Ohio Railway for New York. From there they flew to Luxembourg, and then on to Belgium. The move was an escape from the isolation of their Midwestern American lives rather than a conscious avoidance of the draft and the growing American involvement in Vietnam. "There was no talk about resisting the draft. Ironton is a Midwestern town with Midwestern values. I wasn't all fired up against the war. To me, you basically trusted the government to do the right thing," John recalls.

The move back to Belgium, however, did little to alleviate the family's problems. John's mother had lost her citizenship and couldn't get a work permit, and they found it difficult to readjust to the prescribed Belgian ways. Learning that Canada was accepting more and more immigrants, John and his mother contacted the Canadian embassy. "All they wanted to know was if you were healthy and a person of good character. They lent us money and we moved to Montreal. Within four days of arriving, Mom had a job as a proofreader. A few days later I became a clerk at Northern Electric. While there I became a draftsman, and that's how I got into the technical field."

In 1968 John started night school at Sir George Williams University – today known as Concordia – studying science. When he was laid off from his job in 1982, he used the opportunity to complete his bachelor's degree full-time. In 1988 he sold his brother a half share of his Montreal home in order to finance a master of science degree in urban planning.

By this time John was a confirmed Canadian and no longer had a "criminal file" in the United States. In October 1974 he had received one of many similar letters mailed to Canadian addresses by the U.S. Department of Justice. John's letter, signed by U.S. Attorney William W. Milligan of the southern district of Ohio, is referenced: "United States v. John Michael Thompson, Criminal File No. 11378." It states:

> This letter concerns reports received by this office that you have committed an offense against the United States on or about July 24, 1968, in violation of Section 12 of the Military Selective Service Act.
>
> In accord with the President's policy of granting leniency to certain individuals who are charged with violating Section 12 of the Military Selective Service Act, you are eligible for diversion to an alternate service program. Should you agree to undertake acceptable alternate service as an acknowledgment of your allegiance to the United States, this office will refrain from prosecution. Note, however, that if no agreement is reached, the United States will be free to prosecute you for the Section 12 charge. If the Director of Selective Service certifies

to us that you have successfully completed your service, the pending charge against you will be dropped. However, failure satisfactorily to complete the alternate service will probably cause us to resume prosecution of the Section 12 charge.

The decision to seek acceptance into this program is one that must ultimately be made by you. Nevertheless, it is important that you immediately discuss this matter with your attorney inasmuch as your participation in this program will require a waiver of certain rights afforded to you by the Constitution. For example, you must waive your right to a speedy trial and right to have an indictment presented to the grand jury, if one has not already been obtained, within the prescribed statute of limitations. We suggest that you consult with your attorney who will explain the program to you and the nature of the waivers mentioned above.

John replied immediately to Milligan, pointing out that the charges should be dropped because he had never actually refused induction and, if he had been processed in the usual manner, he would have been found unfit for service due to his rheumatic heart condition. He went on to say:

As to the phrasing in your letter, "criminal file," I object to this as a defamation of my good character. My character is beyond reproach. The application of the term "criminal" in reference to me is ludicrous. I demand you refrain from including this term in your future correspondence. I had no complicity with a system that itself committed heinous crimes against humanity. Furthermore, I do not wish to involve myself in a political trade-off regarding a certain disreputable personality. I find the conditions for leniency onerous beyond belief. I shall never waive my right to a "speedy" trial, and, indeed, it would be "speedy." The case would summarily be dismissed.

I add, in closing, that my only interest in this offer of leniency is the chance to clear my name. I deny any wrongdoing. If I ever must choose between the United States and

Canada, I will choose Canada. I should never choose to suffer the ordure of American life and its political system.

On February 4, 1975, when Assistant U.S. Attorney Anthony W.
Nyktas replied for Milligan, the reference number had been abbrevi-
ated from "Criminal" to "Cr." The brief, single paragraph said: "This
will advise that the Indictment returned by the Federal Grand Jury
against you on July 24, 1968, was dismissed in U.S. District Court on
February 3, 1975. I have so advised the U.S. Marshal and the Federal
Bureau of Investigation and dismissed all warrants of arrest based on
the said Indictment. A certified copy of the Order for Dismissal is
enclosed for your records."

John Thompson is still bemused by the presumption of the
American officials, but none of it plays a very large part in his life today.
Currently he is employed with the Toronto Transit Commission as a
senior estimator. He is intensely involved with an innovative light-rail
transit project that will take Toronto streetcars below ground to allow
the speedy transfer of people from the subway station at Bloor and
Spadina. It is one of those urban projects that takes a very long time to
complete, costs millions of dollars, and gives people something to
grouse about. John clearly loves it all.

CHARLES BELCHER

Not a Saltwater Yankee

WHAT DOES CHARLES BELCHER like most about Canada? "There's a peacefulness and a sense of safety in Canada that you don't find in the States. When I first deserted from the army and came up here, it immediately reminded me of my hometown, Newark, back in the 1950s before the riots. In those days, hard as it is to imagine now, there was a sort of innocence in the black inner city." For Charles, then, coming to Canada was a little like going home to a gentler time.

Historically it has been the aristocracy that declares wars and the underclasses that fight them. In Vietnam's case, of course, the rich white establishment didn't even bother declaring war before it sent off thousands of working-class kids to fight. Of those kids a dispro-portionate number were black. In her excellent 1984 account, *Long*

Time Passing: Vietnam and the Haunted Generation, Myra MacPherson says: "Although under-represented in the armed services as a whole, blacks still accounted for 16 percent of combat deaths from 1961 to 1966. In 1965 . . . 23.5 percent of all Army enlisted men killed in action were black. . . . While blacks averaged about 9.3 percent of total active-duty personnel in 1965-70, they suffered 12.6 percent of the deaths – 30 percent in excess of their presence in Indochina."

For working-class kids, white or black, the military was often seen as a way to participate as an American citizen while obtaining steady employment. However, when Charles was growing up in the friendly but tough streets of Newark, New Jersey, in the 1950s, he wasn't thinking about a military career. His dad had left the family, but he had an abundance of relatives to make up for that. Charles was the second oldest of 49 cousins and lived with his resilient grandmother who had moved up north from Virginia to become "ward of the block." When his mother remarried and moved out to the suburb of Roselle, Charles was amazed at all the green: "I hadn't seen grass like that in Newark except for a few parks. To me the city was basically streets."

The move was important for more than the grass. It showed young Charles that African-Americans could take control of their lives, an idea that was supported by his mother's teachings and her expectations of him in his school academics and sports. Born in 1949, Charles was 12 when the family bought a lot and built the house in suburbia. These were the early years of the Civil Rights Movement, and "block busting" was a term commonly applied to black families moving into previously white-only neighbourhoods. "There were only two or three other black families on the block when we moved there. The rest were white, so I went to school with white people, which was also a new thing because in the inner city it was all blacks or Puerto Ricans. It was then that I found out that the more grass there was, the fewer black people there were. But the fact that my new neighbourhood was mostly white was really incidental. I wasn't exposed to much racism living in the inner city. Maybe the grown-ups knew more about it because of the economic situation and job limits, but I don't recall a whole lot of that sort of thing."

However, Charles's new suburban school began to show him some of the differences. "I had been on the honour roll almost every year at Morton Street School in Newark. School wasn't all that challenging for me. Then when I moved to the suburbs my grades started to plunge and I realized that going to school in the inner city had been a disadvantage. In Roselle there were children of doctors and lawyers who were already preparing to go to university."

By the time he got to high school, Charles had met the heightened expectations and was taking college prep courses. He had also grown physically toward his full adult size of six feet three inches and 220 pounds. The athletic skills that had been planted by a boys' club in Newark also blossomed in the suburbs. "In Roselle," says Charles, "it meant a lot if a school had good basketball and football teams." So, as a gifted athlete, Charles flourished in his new environment.

In 1967, his senior year in high school, the war in Vietnam was in full swing and evidence of its carnage was finding its way back to Roselle. Charles recalls a visit by U.S. Marines to his neighbourhood: "A friend of mine named Gene Law was killed in Vietnam. Some Marines showed up at his family's door and stayed for the funeral. They were like surrogate family members for a couple of days. On the day of the funeral the Marines dressed up, presented the flag to Gene's mother, did the whole ceremony thing, and then they were gone."

When Charles graduated from high school that year, he was dating a white girl and hoping for an athletic scholarship to Villanova University in Pennsylvania. But his college board marks were too low and he settled for Monmouth College in the coastal town of West Long Branch, New Jersey. In his first year there he played basketball with the varsity team, which took him south to Florida and north to Maine on road trips. His confidence was riding high, and in his second year he began working toward a teaching degree.

Like most blacks of the era, Charles remembers exactly what he was doing on April 4, 1968, the day Martin Luther King, Jr., was assassinated. "That night I was home on a visit and there was a big gathering up on the corner of Ninth Avenue and Spruce in Roselle. The liquor store, the bar, and the sweetshop are there. This was the main corner for black people in the neighbourhood. We just called it the Corner. It was a pretty big crowd and you could feel that something important was happening. It was a kind of community sharing thing going on. Then the police arrived and this big black cop got out of the car and bellowed, 'Okay, gimme the Corner!' But nobody moved, so he called for backup. Next thing, a couple more police cars pulled up and the black cop called for the Corner again. Finally someone in the back of the crowd yelled, 'Hell, no! They killed Martin Luther King tonight! You're not gettin' shit from us!'

"Things got pretty tense. At that moment this woman named Hattie, who lived above a store on the Corner, shouted down from her window, 'Why don't you leave them alone? They're not doin' nothin'.' We were all amazed because Hattie was always calling the cops on us when we hung out on the Corner, and here she was sticking up for us. Well, the cops backed off and that was it." What Charles doesn't say is that he came very close to being involved in the kind of rioting that spread like wildfire across the country in cities small and large.

In the late sixties the civil disobedience and nonviolence of King had begun to give way to increasing militancy with the rise of groups such as the Black Panthers. However, the Panthers weren't a major factor at Charles's college, where only a scant 60 students were black in a population of 5,000. "We were totally integrated at Monmouth and most of the guys had white girlfriends," says Charles. "We were into the hippie movement, like Jimi Hendrix."

But all was not love and peace in Charles's life. His white girlfriend came down from Roselle and they got married. They were pretty hard up financially, especially when they had a son. "I wasn't ready for that," he now says. "I wanted to see the world, so I joined the military. I remember going with my uncle and wife down to Newark to be sworn into the Marines. I was escaping the responsibility of having a baby and being married. I thought the military life would give her security, but I'd still be able to leave New Jersey, travel the world, satisfy some of the tastes of a 19-year-old, and still have money to send home to take care of my son."

In late 1969 the Marines were happy to get a fit fellow like Charles, and they quickly shipped him off to boot camp on Parris Island, South Carolina. Charles found the physical side of boot camp fun, but the psychological games were a different matter. The Marines relentlessly drilled one thing into every recruit: don't think, just follow orders, no matter what they are. The kind of analysis and critical thinking that were prerequisites for any college kid who wanted to succeed were ruthlessly crushed in a Marine boot camp. One example of how chilling this kind of training can be made a deep impression on Charles: "Several weeks into boot camp news of an antiwar demonstration planned for Washington, D.C., filtered into Parris Island. Some of us were standing outside the chow hall at lunch time reading in the newspapers about hippies marching on Washington and how Marines at Camp Lajeune were on alert. One guy, who three or four weeks earlier had been a hippie himself, said, 'Boy, I sure wish I was in Lajeune so I could use my bayonet technique in Washington.' Right there I saw how easily this system had torn these people down and given them a new identity and philosophy so that they were ready to inflict pain, not just on the Vietnamese, but on Americans, too. This was the beginning of the erosion of my military career."

After boot camp and some further advanced infantry training, Charles was posted to a naval base in Georgia, where he experienced the kind of blatant racism he had known little of during his childhood days in Newark. "A bunch of the guys, black and white, went out and drove past a bar. I told them to stop and they tried to talk me out of it, but we stopped, anyway. I walked into the bar and tried to get some take-out food but the bartender just ignored me. Finally I slammed the bar counter and asked, 'Could I get some service down here?' Next thing I knew, the guy reached under the bar, pulled out a shotgun, pointed it toward me, and said, 'We're closed.' A chill came over me and I forgot all about being in the Marine Corps. All I could think about was that I was looking down the barrel of a gun and nobody was laughing. So I backed off, walked out the door, and got back into our car. The other guys didn't say a word."

It was also in Georgia that Charles's appreciation of the Black Panthers began to develop. When some members of the Panthers were raided and shot by police in Chicago, he really began to wonder what he was doing in the military. "Here I was being employed by the government, the same establishment that was killing Black Panthers, members of my race, in the same country that I was going to defend." At about this time Charles started having Black Panther literature mailed to him from an ex-Marine and Vietnam vet in New Jersey. At college he had heard Black Panthers give speeches, but now the meaning of their words were taking on new dimensions.

Rampant racism in Vietnam was seriously affecting the U.S. war effort by this time. In addition to an overall dissatisfaction with their role in the military, blacks figured prominently in the increasing incidence of "fragging," deadly attacks on officers by enlisted men, usually with grenades. Myra MacPherson reports that fraggings "increased enormously from 1969 to 1970. In 1969 there were 96 documented assaults; in 1970 there were 209." Charles saw the military's response to this sort of problem when a race relations officer arrived on the base to give lectures against fragging. At the same time returning vets supplied ample proof of the emotional scars one could receive in an unpopular war.

One night Charles and a white friend were on guard duty when they got a call to go and pick up a local black Vietnam veteran who had gone AWOL. The vet was delivered to the gates of the compound in handcuffs by a pair of MPs. "We took him upstairs to the lieutenant to be interrogated. He had on this black leather Mau Mau bracelet that blacks in Vietnam wore as a symbol of fraternity. The white lieutenant told me to cut the bracelet off, but I wouldn't. Then my buddy roughed the prisoner up and cut the bracelet off. When we got outside, he asked, 'What are you doing? The lieutenant's watching you, so you got to act mean. You got to play the role.'"

Shortly after this incident Charles decided he had had enough. Packing a bag, he left the base and headed home to his wife back in West Long Branch. He stayed there for a couple of months while the authorities looked for him in Roselle. For a while life almost seemed normal and he was able to spend a lot of time with his toddler son on the beach. He even made a little money by using his military ID to buy low-cost cigarettes at the nearby Fort Monmouth PX and selling them at regular prices after the bars closed. At first he planned to go to Trinidad but then changed his mind and decided to go to Canada. When he told his grandmother that he was leaving the country, she said, "You won't be the first one in the family. In World War II we had a cousin who went to England and we ain't never heard from him since."

That was the most support Charles got from his family. His wife's parents were upset about her marrying a black man and having a child while still a teenager. His mother kept trying to get him to return to the Marines and even asked a friend who was a World War II vet to talk some "sense" into him. All the while the FBI continued hunting for him in Roselle. Twice, when he was visiting his mother, they missed him by just a few minutes. Another time they arrested his uncle by mistake.

Charles endured all of this and continued with his plans. "I was reading a *Playboy* magazine one night and I saw a story on the Montreal Playboy Club, and in one of the photos there was a black guy. I thought, Well, if they're civilized enough to have a Playboy Club and there's already one black guy up there, then what the hell, maybe I should go there. My neighbour's church was planning a bus trip to Montreal, so I told them that I wanted a ticket but wouldn't be returning to New Jersey. When we hit the border, they took some kid and put him under the seats so that when the customs guy counted he got the right head count. When the church group went back to the States, they just put the kid back in my place."

It was the summer of 1970 in Montreal and at first Charles stayed in hostels. Then he contacted some people at McGill University who told him he would be better off in Toronto since he didn't speak French. "I spent my last $12 on the bus ticket," he recalls. Toronto proved to be a good place for the young deserter. Naomi Wells of the Toronto Antidraft Program arranged places for him to stay and helped him find some temporary work. "It was great. I was free and all that, but there was no substance. I didn't have a real job and I had no connection with society. Other deserters and draft dodgers were my friends. We were all pretty much together in spirit, but deserters, like myself, knew they were definitely going to Leavenworth for some hard time if they were caught back in the States."

Even Canada didn't feel entirely safe from the long arm of Uncle Sam. "There was a lot of paranoia about who you told your name to. There was talk about the FBI being in Toronto and stories about people they had tracked down and kidnapped back to the States. So I stayed away from the anti-establishment scene at Rochdale College, the hippie hangout. If the FBI wanted to find me, that was the first place they'd look."

Without landed immigrant status and a social insurance number it was impossible for Charles to work legally. One day he and several other draft dodgers and deserters were working for a Canadian who had a franchise to sell brushes door-to-door when they were arrested. The police had mistaken them for a ring of house robbers, and Charles prepared himself for the worst when they discovered he was a deserter. He got a surprise, though. "One of the cops pointed at another cop and said, 'See that guy sitting over there? He's a deserter from the Irish army. And that guy's a deserter from the Hungarian army.' It turned out that about six cops in that station were deserters from various armies all around the world. They told us that it was great that we weren't doing anything really illegal but that we'd better get our papers organized as soon as possible to make things legal. One of the cops who was going off duty even gave us a ride back to our car. I think it was then that I really began to feel that Canada was all right. People really seemed to have common sense."

The Toronto Antidraft Program made arrangements for Charles to enter the country legally so that he could get landed immigrant status. "They sent me to this priest's home in Windsor. I stayed there overnight and he gave me $500. Then he and I crossed the border into Detroit. I went to a bar to buy cigarettes and the bartender gave me the wrong change, so I started to argue with him until I realized I was back in the States and the FBI was looking for me. Well, I beat it out of the bar and the priest and I went back to the border where I applied for landed immigrant status. I had a letter promising me a job in Toronto, I had the $500, and I had three years of university, so I passed and they stamped me landed immigrant. After that I returned the $500 to the priest, thanked him a lot, and headed back to Toronto. Things started to pick up for me then."

Eventually Charles's wife came up to Toronto with their son, and for a while they tried to put things back together, but it didn't work out and his wife returned to the States with their son. In spite of the FLQ crisis in Quebec, which reminded Charles of the Newark riots, the early 1970s were a time of optimism in Canada. The government seemed to have faith that young people were an asset to the nation and encouraged innovative job creation through projects like the Local Initiatives Program (LIP). "One of the first decent jobs I had was working on one of the LIP projects with an organization called the Black Community Action Committee. It was set up in the city's west end YMCA and run by a couple of well-off Trinidadian guys. They helped foster action on integration cases, school liaison, and community activities for the black community."

Charles's participation in the black community of Toronto was not without its cultural conflicts. "The West Indians felt as though they were the real blacks and that they weren't so influenced by the whites as black Canadians were. As a black American, I felt like I was in the middle, sort of a mediator between the two groups. I never really did assimilate into West Indian culture. When I first went to Toronto, the West Indians called me a 'saltwater Yankee,' which to them was a West Indian who went to the States and returned to the West Indies speaking like an American. What they were saying was, 'We know you from the West Indies so why you talking like an American?'" Charles felt some resentment at that, but appreciates, as many whites do not, that black society in Canada, or anywhere else for that matter, is not monolithic.

Eventually, though, Charles found a place for himself in Toronto's West Indian community. The LIP project developed into a four-year grant that allowed Charles and his colleagues to open the Harriet Tubman Youth Centre, which was named after the black woman who operated the Underground Railroad that brought a much earlier generation of American blacks to Canada. Charles became the centre's recreational supervisor and coached a basketball team that toured Barbados, Trinidad, Antigua, and Guyana. This work led to other recreational and child-care work with the Toronto Children's Aid Society.

Throughout this time Charles kept in touch with the Toronto Antidraft Program. which told him about the amnesty for deserters. "A bunch of us travelled down to Fort Benjamin Harrison in Indiana, stood in line, and got processed. They gave me back pay, a dishonourable discharge, and a plane ticket to Newark. I could have gotten a general discharge, though, if I'd agreed to work for 22 months at a veterans' hospital near Lansing, Michigan, but I didn't bother."

When Charles returned to Canada, he continued working in the West Indian community with others who were striving to unify the diverse black cultures within Toronto. He also worked with ex-convicts on probation and with emotionally disturbed children. In 1994, after more than two decades in Toronto, he married again and moved to Vancouver, where he is now employed in the psychiatric department of the B.C. Children's Hospital. A daughter, Jamillah, from a former relationship with a woman of West Indian descent, lives with Charles and his new wife.

"You know," Charles says at the end of our long talk, the weight of too many memories obvious in his face, "my son now lives in Arizona. He once told me he'd rather I'd gone to Vietnam and died than have gone to Canada. With Gail's help I'm trying to get closer to him." Charles may not have really found the innocence of his youth in Canada, but he does seem to have discovered some kind of inner peace, one that may well be quintessentially Canadian.

NORM SIBUM

Poet as Outsider

NORM SIBUM HAS PUBLISHED several volumes of his poetry in England and in Canada, and his work has recently been included in a CD-ROM anthology. But one of his most significant, and memorable, moments of recognition came from a small-town bar in Washington State. "My father was living in a flophouse and drinking out of Budweiser cans in Centralia. But he had set up court in the local bar and used to pass my poems around. I was up here in Canada and I was not doing well. I was broke. I was trying to write. I didn't know who I was. I was going through women. But there, in that little bar, I was famous."

It was a bad time and, needing an antidote for his depression, Norm took the woman he was with at the time and went to visit his father. "He was so gracious and civilized, and I realized, even in his dingy little room, that I loved him. He had made a kind of peace with himself. Such is America. All things are possible."

Norm's father spent much of his life outside mainstream American society and, while their lives have followed very different courses, Norm and his father did share a sense of apartness from other people. When his father died, he and his sisters held a wake for him in that little hotel, and the experience brought Norm one step closer to accepting his position in life as an outsider. It is a good place, perhaps the only place, for a poet to be – outside looking in – and it is a place where Norm, like his father, has spent most of his life.

When he was 12 years old, Norm's father emigrated from Germany to the United States in the 1930s. He had come over to join his parents in Pennsylvania but immediately left them and went to Brooklyn to live on his own. Drafted into the U.S. Army to fight in World War II, he protested that he couldn't go and shoot his own people. Fortunately the army gave him an intelligence posting. When the war was over, he managed an officers' club in Oberammergau, a village near Munich. It was there that this young man from a German-peasant background met and married a woman of the Berlin bourgeoisie. She had danced in the 1936 Olympics in Berlin when Hitler had showcased Aryan youth. During the Allied bombardment of Berlin, she fled to Prague and joined the American forces coming into Germany from the south. The young couple were still living on an army base in Germany when Norm was born in 1947.

The family stayed on in Europe until Norm's father was transferred to Fort Richardson, Alaska. Norm loved Alaska, but his mother hated it there and felt that the American women on the base had no appreciation of her sophisticated background. "Here she is with this German hick, now her husband, who is also an American. It was very hard for her," recalls Norm. "My father had all these get-rich-quick schemes that always fell apart. My mother would say, 'That's your father for you.' It was hard on me."

The family stayed in Alaska until Norm was in the fourth grade, and then his father, who was still in the military, was transferred back to Germany. Once they had settled in Germany again, Norm began to meet his mother's family and started to identify with his German heritage. "I had the unique experience of knowing what it was like to be both colonial and colonized," says Norm.

It was this sense of being two things at once – a kind of double-consciousness – that set Norm apart from so many of his schoolmates and created a gulf between him and his parents. In the early sixties Norm's father left the army and attempted to live a civilian life. Norm describes that time in his poem "Export A's," taken from *Small Commerce*, an early collection of verse:

> . . . i think of my father. who wore
> such slack clothes, after a
> lifetime in the army, and
> came apart, and it was not
> even slow. unravelled into
> a useless skein of skin, bone,
> jesus, after the fantasy
> of a lifetime, the occupation
> of germany. meaningless chore . . .

In 1964, just before Norm's father left the military, he was transferred from Germany to Utah. and then to Fort Lewis in Washington State. The family lived in the nearby state capital of Olympia, and Norm started hanging out at the Null-Set Coffee House, which was run by a couple of beat generation left-wing types from Boston and featured a lot of poetry readings. Since Norm's father had left the army, family life had gone from bad to worse. So, at only 16, Norm struck out on his own for Seattle. For a year he moved back and forth between Olympia and Seattle, listening to poetry at the Null-Set and Seattle's Pike Place Market and serving a kind of poetic apprenticeship in both places. "I was living in the basement of the Null-Set and surviving on handouts from the Unitarian wives," Norm recalls ruefully.

More a beat poet than a hippie, Norm was reading Federico García Lorca and trying to understand the Spanish Civil War. It was his coming-of-age summer – when war stopped being something that only took place 30 years earlier in Spain, and when his friend Billy was drafted. By the time Billy had completed his basic training, Norm was about to be inducted himself. Billy had a paper route and came to agonize with Norm over whether or not he should go to Vietnam.

"He got suicidal. One afternoon, inviting me to help him deliver the papers, he tried to kill both of us, doing 110 fucking miles an hour on a country road. I had to reach over and grab the wheel. He cried. Then we decided that the weekend before he actually had to leave for Vietnam we were going to have this wild time in a hotel room with a girl we both loved. All three of us were still virgins. Billy was this fat, unkempt sort of kid, and my mother thought he was a homosexual and that I was involved with him. At that point I got mad and told her I wasn't homosexual and I wasn't going to the war." Having spent most of her adult years living in a military community, Norm's mother was shocked by his decision not to go to Vietnam.

The weekend in the hotel was both anticlimactic and poignant. "There were the three of us, lying on this bed, going through all this stuff," Norm recalls. "We were very close. There were no parents. Nothing. We were utterly alone in the universe." In the end nobody had sex with anyone, but the three young friends lay together on the bed and looked into their diverse futures. Billy did end up going to Vietnam and returned a bitter and cynical man. No one knows what happened to the girl. As for Norm, that weekend he confirmed his decision not to go to war.

"That was a hell of a summer," says Norm as he remembers the wild ride of emotions that arose around his decision not to follow Billy off to war. "I was bewildered. I was confused. At certain times I felt almost sanctimonious, even politically righteous. At times I felt guilty, because I'd think, Am I a coward? I understood that my mother was trying to make me feel bad. She was the strong force in the family, but I felt that she was being a hypocrite, and I lost respect for her. I knew she was embarrassed about what the neighbours would think. I felt that, ultimately, she wasn't interested in my welfare. She was interested in her own."

Norm's father, only in his forties at the time, was working at a gas station and becoming a serious alcoholic. But his reaction to Norm's decision not to go to war was very different than his wife's. Sometime after the pivotal weekend that Norm spent in the hotel room with his friends, his father tracked him down at the Null-Set and suggested they talk. It was a brief conversation and Norm's father avoided moralizing. Rather, he looked at Norm and said, "To tell you the truth, I'd just as soon you didn't go to Vietnam, because they're incompetent over there. If you're going to be killed, I don't want it to be because some idiot doesn't know how to run an army." Eventually Norm's mother also came to accept his decision not to go to Vietnam.

Norm's weekend of innocence in the hotel with his friends was quickly left behind when he married a woman in her early twenties. Enrolled at the University of Washington in Seattle, he still spent a lot of time at the Pike Place Market. "I loved that place. For me, the soul of the world was right there, and I now realize that in that cosmology I became – and this is the only way I can describe it – a Jeffersonian Democrat. I accepted that I wasn't egalitarian. I was an observer going there to watch and hear poets and to learn to write. I also realize now that I was learning my politics there, as well."

But Norm turned 18 and the pressure of the draft grew more intense. After a quick trip to his wife's hometown in Alabama, the couple prepared for Norm's move to Canada. He got a student visa by enrolling at the now-defunct Shurpass Pacific College in Vancouver. He still hadn't been drafted and continued to visit his wife in Seattle, where she worked part-time as a stripper in a black bar in order to provide Norm with a weekly allowance. Norm rented a room from an old Ukrainian Communist named Felix, who broadened the young man's horizons by having him listen to Radio Moscow and plying him with homemade wine laced with vodka. In spite of having lived in Germany for many years with a father who fought to "defend" the West against the Communist threat, Norm was able to accept old Felix and others like him whom he met in Vancouver. He had learned tolerance and mutual respect from his parents, who had a broader European outlook on the world than many of their fellow Americans. Norm remembers his father telling him, "This cold war is just a shell game."

Eventually Norm got a job with Mel Hurtig – who owned a bookstore in Edmonton – and that was enough to secure the landed immigrant status he needed in order to stay in Canada without going to school. After a brief stint in Alberta, he boarded a bus to Vancouver and was welcomed back to the province by two women who masturbated him in the back of a Greyhound bus. It seemed this world, or this part of the world at least, was still innocent.

But back in Vancouver, where his wife had joined him and was working as a keypunch operator, things weren't so welcoming. Jobs were hard to find. Norm had worked at the state library in Olympia shelving legislative documents, reading I. F. Stone, *Harper's, Ramparts,* and so on. Now he went out to the University of British Columbia, hoping to find work at the school's library. "Jerry Rubin was there having a demonstration. I took one look at the whole scene and realized something had changed. Here was this ridiculous asshole trying to radicalize these poor fucking goofball Canadians, and here I was trying to find a job. I was angry. Pissed off."

He finally found work at the Simon Fraser University library but hated the academics he met there, many of whom were Americans. "I realized they were the same people I didn't like in high school. It was only later that I came to understand that it was because they were middle-class and I was working-class." Norm quit his job at the library after six months.

Norm Sibum, the outsider, was now in a foreign country, surrounded by American expatriates of a different social class. It was good for his poetry but hard on his soul. "I was writing a great deal of poetry in places like the Aristocratic Restaurant on Granville, and I would sit there all night long wallowing in my misery and loneliness, nursing a single cup of coffee. I was trying to find a community."

His marriage broke up after his wife ran off with his best friend, a fellow draft dodger, who deliberately got into trouble with the Canadian law so that he would be sent back to the United States. Norm's wife went back with him. In the meantime, Norm was too shy to get into poetry readings in Vancouver, but he was starting to associate with a community of poets that included George Bowering, Patrick Lane, David Phillips, Ken Balford, Barry McKinnon, and Howard White. It was one member of this group, Barry McKinnon, who first published Norm in Canada in 1972. In this community Norm could comfortably sit in, but he remained conscious that he was very different. Nevertheless, it was an extremely lonely time for Norm. Even in *Small Commerce*, his second book, he is still clearly dissatisfied with his life and laments in "Export A's" that

> after ten years of life in Canada
> after the Vietnam pre-occupation.
> i finally decide on Export A's.
> and try to get born somewhere.

Being a draft dodger wasn't all bad, Norm notes wryly: "I used it as my shtick to pick up girls after my wife left me and I was working in a pizza joint. Being an American and a draft dodger had some currency, and the girls, I'm sorry to say, fell for it almost every time."

Norm hung out on the edges of the Vancouver hippie scene, but he couldn't get rid of the feeling that it was all a farce. "I had a great LSD experience, but I was also having some bad drug trips. I couldn't even smoke grass without having some sort of episode. Then I felt guilty about not being hip. I felt worse about not being hip than

I did about having evaded the draft!"

By the time of the American withdrawal from Vietnam in 1973, Norm was paying more attention to Canada's charismatic Prime Minister Trudeau. "I had a dream that Trudeau was talking to me in the White Lunch Cafeteria on Hastings Street. I was politically naive, very much so, but Trudeau wanted to talk about the 'Canadian soul' and thought he had located part of it there in that dreary diner. I don't know who was putting who on, and I knew he was a politician, but it didn't seem as if he was trying to sell me something, like Nixon and LBJ."

Shortly after the amnesty in 1977, Norm crossed the border with a friend in his old Dodge pickup. "We went to Seattle. Guilt and paranoia hit me like a ton of bricks. Everywhere I went I felt like they knew I was a draft dodger. You know, it's still the same today. When I'm in the States, I'd just as soon not talk about it, although I've had every reaction from sympathy to hostility."

Today, in a manner that could be considered typically Canadian, Norm still searches for an identity. "When you are a writer, you should attack or defend or do something with what is around you – the people, the landscape. In Canada I don't feel I have a right to do that. John Steinbeck could be John Steinbeck because he *was* a Californian. But I don't feel as if Canadians are my people. An old friend of mine, a Canadian who has lived all over the world, asked me why I came up here. I told her it was because I felt deeply interfered with. She said that that made me an American because nobody else in the world is capable of saying such a thing. So I guess I am an American, although in a rather abstract way."

Norm got his Canadian citizenship in 1975. Now, whenever he goes to England to read from his works of poetry, he doesn't know whether to introduce himself as an American or a Canadian poet. "But there are a number of people there," Norm admits, "who read me and don't care what I am." In the past five years Norm has spent a lot of time reading from his work in Europe. His British publisher, after much deliberation over the matter, has decided to identify him as a Canadian poet.

MICHAEL GOLDBERG

First Generation Activist

"I DIDN'T INHERIT my activism from my parents," says Michael Goldberg when asked how he began a life committed to social change. Born in 1943, Michael and his twin brother, Mitchell, grew up in the same lower-middle-class neighbourhood in Denver, Colorado. Researchers have shown that twins raised in different environments display marked similarities in behaviour, yet these twin brothers couldn't have turned out more different from each other. Later in life, while Michael devoted himself to counselling draft dodgers and deserters from the Vietnam War, Mitchell was dedicated to recruiting men into the U.S. Army.

After experiencing difficulties with their mother and the death of their father when they were only 17 years old, the boys went to live with their maternal grandparents, who were Jewish immigrants from eastern Europe: "They didn't have any education," Michael recalls, "but they were very bright people. We also found out much later in life that they were more giving people than we had ever realized. For example, they funded a young black woman's education and she is now dean of a university."

Undoubtedly the example of these immigrant grandparents, who ran a small grocery store in one of Denver's poorer neighbourhoods, had a profound influence on Michael. His grandfather had come to the United States on his own at the age of 12 when most of his family had been killed in the pogroms in the Ukraine. "I grew up in a Jewish community on the west side of town when all the more well-off Jews were moving to the east side. Our life was definitely not affluent."

Michael attended school with children from a variety of ethnic backgrounds – European, Mexican, African-American. It was this exposure that first opened his eyes to the injustices inherent in American society. Even in elementary school the bud of his activist organizational skills had begun to form, and Michael felt the first stirrings of his political questioning of the status quo. "I tended to be just a little more political than Mitchell and was elected president of the student council for one term in grade six. My brother ran the next term, but only made vice president."

After the twins' high school graduation in 1961, Michael went off to Monmouth College in Illinois on a scholarship, while his brother stayed in Colorado to attend the state university in Boulder. "I organized the Young Democrats on that *very* Republican campus," he recalls. "It was radical to be a Democrat at Monmouth. But it was also there that I first experienced anti-Semitism."

Michael stayed at Monmouth only until his second year when "too much card playing" began to interfere with his studies. In 1963 he returned to Denver to live with his grandparents and enrolled in night classes at the University of Colorado, where his brother was a full year ahead of him and had already married his high school sweet-heart. Michael was "going through a late adolescence," but he was, through some of the young night school professors, beginning to develop a strong political consciousness. In fact, his first involvement in an anti-establishment demonstration was with the Caesar Chavez California grape boycott.

Michael continued to work on the grape boycott, but his interest was piqued by a new group that called itself the Students for a Democratic Society (SDS). It had issued its first manifesto at Ann Arbor, Michigan, in 1963, and Michael and a few others began organizing a chapter of the SDS in Denver the following year. "A side benefit of forming the SDS chapter was that the university had a rule that all organizations could have a table set up on the concourse of the student union building every other week. A lot of us were selling buttons and stuff at our table to try to educate the campus. Then we formed an alliance with the Student Peace Movement (SPM) so that we were ensured a table every week. But I felt that the SPM was too church-based. It came out of the Quaker movement and the people involved were very sincere, but the group just wasn't sufficiently activist for my taste. The SDS had a much broader political agenda."

Each year student protests on campus increased. In Michael's first year at the University of Colorado the usual protest marches took place. But in his second year a larger protest happened to coincide with the university's big homecoming football game. The organization planned to take a somewhat more innovative approach: "We decided to reach a different audience. Using one of the writers from the student newspaper, who was a great satirist, we produced a flyer with the team's starting lineup on one side and, on the other side, we printed a satire called 'The Bigger Game: Coming Home.' Using football jargon, it told about the war in Vietnam and the American threat to use nuclear weapons there. We handed them out at the game to a captive audience of 45,000. We also got tickets to the game – 15 seats right under the scoreboard. One of our other people constructed three-by-five-foot cards with a letter on each one. Every time a point was scored, the 15 people below the scoreboard would hold up the cards to spell PEACE IN VIETNAM, and then they would flip them over to spell out NEGOTIATE NOW! When we raised the cards the first time, there was a chorus of boos but, after a while, people just got used to the messages being there. The whole thing was captured in a picture in *Newsweek*." It was activities such as these that helped earn the University of Colorado the distinction of being one of a small group of schools identified as hotbeds of dissent by the House Un-American Activities Committee in 1966.

In the midst of all these demonstrations Michael's twin brother was working toward a law degree and was active in the campus Reserve Officer Training Corps (ROTC). When it was announced that the ROTC's annual ball was going to be held in one of the town's better hotels, Michael and his cohorts went into action. They began by leaking to the press that they were planning a major protest against the event. When the hotel management became worried and decided to cancel the ball, Michael's group promised that they wouldn't do anything to damage property. "One of the things we did was obtain a case of fortune cookies and, one at a time, we took the fortunes out with tweezers and inserted new ones, each one hand-typed. We delivered the cookies and a guy dressed as a waiter distributed them. When the ROTC officers opened their fortunes after dinner, they each got their own antiwar slogan. That night, at 2:00 a.m., the ROTC commandant phoned to acknowledge that we had duped him. But the faculty military officer wanted to have us banned from campus, and we got four more days of press because of that."

In about 1966 the situation was heating up in Vietnam and in the antiwar movement at home. The Colorado SDS chapter decided to stage a 48-hour fast for peace on the university library steps. It was late in the fall and bitterly cold. As the little group of students sat shivering on the steps, the campus branch of the Young Republicans arrived to throw snowballs at the fasters. "In the meantime," says

Michael, "word had gone out over the campus radio station about how cold and wet we were. Then students began bringing plastic bottles of hot water to help keep us warm."

The next day the Young Republicans and the Young Americans for Freedom returned, this time with barbecues on which they cooked hamburgers to give away in front of the fasting students. But their plan backfired again when neither the fasters nor the passing students would take any food. "No one would touch the food, and the students walking by were saying, 'You assholes.' Their actions served to bring media attention to the event, too." The tactics employed by Michael's organization were not exactly in keeping with Gandhi's ascetic passivism, but they were clever, active approaches to nonviolent confrontation. "In the early sixties we still weren't particularly militant. People were starting to become impatient and I had to remind them that we'd lose the battle if we started becoming assholes like them."

Michael was involved in another demonstration that placed him in direct opposition to his twin brother, who was now a captain in the ROTC. This was a protest against the ROTC's recruiting efforts. One warm fall day when Mitchell and his cadets were drilling on the football field, Michael, the long-haired hippie, stood on the opposite side of the field with a ragtag bunch of students who were offering cold soft drinks to the young men. This was done in an effort to entice the cadets over for a talk on how their involvement in the ROTC was helping the war effort.

Michael and his brother managed to maintain cordial relations throughout all of this: "He respected my position, even though I didn't respect his at all. He wanted to be a lawyer, and being in the reserves was a way to pay for that. He didn't believe in the war in an America-Love-It-or-Leave-It sense, but he felt that he had made his commitments and had some obligations to fulfill. He also believed that the war wasn't all bad, whereas I believed that the war was not only morally wrong, but that there was nothing to be gained from its geopolitical positioning."

Michael became more and more proficient at organizing people into nonviolent political movements while gaining the best possible media attention. Then, one day in 1966, while working at an information booth next to one of the Peace Corps', he was recruited. The fellow in the Peace Corps booth kept hassling Michael: "You guys are all talk and no action. Why don't you get out in the real world where you can make a difference to others?" To get the fellow off his back, Michael filled out an application and answered the question on why he wanted to join the Peace Corps with, "To avoid the draft." To the question on where he would want to be posted, he answered, "Anywhere a radical would feel comfortable."

To his amazement, Michael received notice a short time later that he had been accepted into the Peace Corps. This coincided with the termination of his student deferment, even though he was just beginning his fourth year of university. In spite of the fact that the recruiting office finally acknowledged that he was still a student and agreed to put a hold on his military call-up, Michael saw this as an obvious attempt to manipulate someone who was assuming an activist role in opposing the war. So he decided to go to the Peace Corps training session, which was held at the University of Wisconsin in Milwaukee, but he didn't feel that he fitted in with the bright-eyed young students who were hoping to make a contribution in rural India. "I was with a bunch of button-down fraternity and sorority kids," he says, "and I had this massive head of hair."

Then, when a process that the Peace Corps trainers called "peer selection" was introduced, Michael attempted to organize an internal boycott. Each person was asked to name five individuals of the 80 present who they thought should go abroad and five who they thought should not. It looked as if the boycott was going to hold when, "On the morning of the final day, the head of the Peace Corps in Washington made an appearance and said that anyone who didn't participate in the peer selection process would automatically be dismissed. We had virtually a 100 percent lock on it, but that killed it right there."

Michael was the only one who didn't participate in the peer selection, but his director spoke on his behalf and, in 1967, he was assigned to northern India. The program director there had already heard of Michael and tried, unsuccessfully, to have him diverted to Latin America. By this time Michael was having his doubts about the whole thing: "I decided to travel across Canada to see whether I would want to move there if the Corps didn't work out and I lost my deferment. I knew that I didn't want to go to jail because you couldn't organize shit there, and I definitely knew that I didn't want to go to Vietnam. I was also aware that I wouldn't qualify for conscientious objector status."

Crossing the border into Manitoba, Michael drove across western Canada and liked what he saw. In Vancouver he was offered a youth counselling position at the Jewish Community Centre, but turned it down to fulfill his commitment in India. His time in the Peace Corps, however, was short-lived: "After four months in India, it became really apparent that I wasn't going to survive in the Corps, so they gave me an offer that I couldn't refuse. Normally if you left early you had to pay your own airfare home. They offered to both pay me and provide me with a plane ticket if I would leave right then and there."

Michael flew back to Denver and attended an SDS meeting the night that he got home. Within 24 hours he received a notice to report to his draft board. He called the Jewish Community Centre in Vancouver and found that the job they had offered him was still available. Arriving at the border crossing in Blaine, Washington, just south of Vancouver, on October 8, 1967, Michael was one of the first people to enter Canada under the new point system that had been implemented just a week earlier. "The immigration officer had never used the point form before and I had been briefed on the procedure by the American Friends Committee before I left the United States, so I had to walk him through the whole thing. The job offer at the centre automatically gave me 15 points. The last item on the form was on character, and when he asked me what to put down for that one,

I told him that it didn't matter, since I was already over the required 50 out of a possible 100 points."

In Vancouver the Jewish Community Centre provided Michael with some contacts and a place to settle. He also met his wife, Dianne, there, who came from a family that was involved in its own fair share of political activity. After a year as a youth counsellor at the centre, Michael enrolled in a two-year program at the University of British Columbia's School of Social Work. Part of the program involved a practicum, which he arranged to do with the Committee to Aid American War Objectors. He worked as a volunteer counsellor out of their Hastings Street office on Vancouver's east side and then continued in that job for a year after completing his practicum.

It was while advising deserters and dodgers that Michael came up against his brother again: "He had finished law school and was working as an induction officer in Seattle. Young men would go to see him to ask about refusing induction and he would explain that if they did so they would be arrested and placed in a hotel for the night before being arraigned in the morning. Of course, when they were put in the hotel, they would skip out and come to Canada where they would end up in my office.

"Needless to say, my brother and I looked very much alike, but he had a brush cut and I had big, wild hair. I could tell when someone was from Seattle because they would look at me and then grab my hair to see if it was a wig. I would ask them, 'Did you go through induction in Seattle?' And they would panic and ask, 'It is you, isn't it?'" Mitchell ended up doing a tour of duty in Vietnam for a year before returning to civilian life and a law practice in Southern California. He has since been appointed a judge.

For these young people, some of whom had snuck across the border in the middle of the night, the sight of what they thought was their induction officer in a wig just added to their already heightened sense of anxiety. Many of the draft evaders entered Canada legally as visitors but had not applied for landed immigrant status at the border.

It was Michael's job first to determine how many points they could qualify for and then find ways to make up the difference if necessary. One way to do so was to line up a job offer for them, which assured the applicant another 15 points. Duthie Books was one place that would often provide job letters, whether they were in need of staff or not.

Michael is still careful when he tells of some of the activities that were carried out in support of draft evaders and deserters at that time. Some of the deals that were arranged are better left unknown, he maintains, not so much because they bordered on being illegal, but because they could prove to be embarrassing for influential public figures who were involved. "We had people who arranged housing, money, education – whatever was necessary," Michael recalls of those intense times.

In the years after he moved on from the Committee to Aid American War Objectors, Michael worked at the North Shore Neighbourhood House. It was 1970, he had married Dianne by this time, and the couple took the summer off to drive across Canada to St. John's, Newfoundland. It was on this trip that Michael's commitment to Canada was validated. The election of an NDP government in British Columbia further confirmed his understanding of Canada as a country with more political options than the United States. "There is an openness around political issues here that I think many Canadians don't recognize," he says, "and it's sad that they aren't aware of what they have. I guess early on, as a political refugee from another country, I quickly came to appreciate this political context."

After leaving the North Shore Neighbourhood House, Michael worked for the federal government but, just as during his days in the Peace Corps, he became frustrated with the many layers of bureaucracy. In 1973 he took his community organizational skills to work for the British Columbia Association of Nonstatus Indians. "That was an interesting job because it required a lot of work in our nation's capital during the Trudeau era. I remember walking down a street in

Ottawa with our executive director, Fred House, when a car came along with Trudeau inside. He rolled down the window and called out, 'Hi, Fred!' Imagine walking down a street in Washington and having Kennedy or Johnson or Reagan roll down a car window and call out to greet someone! It never would have happened."

In 1977 Michael took a position with the Kiwassa Neighbourhood Services Association. While there he worked on a number of social projects, including one for hearing-impaired children. Then, with their two daughters – born in 1971 and 1975 – the family moved to England, where Michael completed the course work for a Ph.D. Since 1988 he has been the director of research for the nonprofit Social Planning and Research Council of British Columbia. Once again the organizational skills that he gained from his politically active campus days have proved useful in his job of explaining social and justice issues to the media. He has also appeared before both the House of Commons and the Senate Committees to present briefs on social justice concerns. "I've found my place in a mainstream organization and am able to give voice to these important issues," he says with a sense of satisfaction that is clearly justified.

Michael and Dianne's two daughters show every sign of continuing in the activist footsteps of their parents. But the nineties are unlike the sixties in many ways. There are different issues to stand up for and different ways of making that stand. In many ways, however, the process hasn't changed. If individuals wish to safeguard the quality of life of citizens in a democracy, they must use the mass media to reach the greater population. Whereas Michael used banners and sit-ins to gain media attention, his daughter Mira has felt the need for more dramatic, and more confrontational, means of protest. "She was arrested in the Walbran Valley [clearcut logging blockade] for chaining herself to the frame of a car on the logging bridge. It took several hours for them to cut the chains off. She had to defend herself in court for eight days over a two-month period and received a sentence of 30 days in jail that was then suspended to probation and 100 hours of community work. The judge ordered that once the protesters had completed their probationary period they would be granted a conditional discharge so that they wouldn't have criminal records. But now the logging corporation, Fletcher Challenge, is suing them in civil court."

Michael and Dianne are obviously proud of Mira's actions, and she clearly has their support. But her willingness to risk her safety and to lose time in her education causes them to worry about social and political activism in the nineties. "The dilemma that arose between myself and my daughter was: 'How far do you take things?' and 'Do you take them to a point where you end up in court?' She has taken a much more radical approach to issues than we ever did.

"Our younger daughter, Avi," Michael continues, "was a student at Concordia University in Montreal in 1994 and was very involved in demonstrations against groups that were promoting antichoice and homophobic agendas." Both of Michael's daughters are very knowledgeable on issues of class, race, and gender, and assume very strong positions on these subjects. "One thing that I find a bit troubling about this era is that there is less of the subtle humour that was evident in my time. The approaches to today's issues seem so much more serious. The world that we live in now seems to be a meaner place. But we are proud that both Mira and Avi are so politically aware and active."

GERALD WIVIOTT

Making Peace out of War

"I WAS A DOCTOR," says Gerald Wiviott in the living room of his comfortable old house in downtown Montreal, "and I knew I wouldn't be asked to carry a gun, nor would I be put in the position where I'd have to kill people. So I really felt I could do more for the antiwar movement if I went to Vietnam because, as a doctor, I could return to the States and tell people what it was like. That way I'd have more credibility as a spokesperson for the antiwar movement."

In a nation in which freedom fighters supposedly overthrew the yoke of tyranny only to suppress the freedom fighters of another land in another century, paradox may well be unavoidable. Long before Gerry had to face moral dilemmas, though, he was no stranger to paradox. His greatest childhood influence in the male-centred society of the forties and fifties was his Jewish atheist mother. "My father worked for Wonder Bread in Milwaukee, where I was born [in 1941]. At first he had a horse-drawn cart and later a truck. Early each morning he'd head off to the bakery and spend the day doing deliveries. When he got home, he'd be real tired, so the family would have supper together and then he'd go off to sleep. My father was supportive, but he wasn't the kind of role model my mother was. She was a very outspoken woman and had quite unorthodox views."

Early on Gerry learned from his mother that there were those who did things properly and those who didn't. "My mother saw the world populated by two kinds of people – Nazis and Jews. I was raised with a strong Jewish identity but without any sense of Jewish tradition or spirituality. My mother explained that she wanted me to have my bar mitzvah so that I could then be free to make my own choice.

"Being an atheist back then was not unlike being a Communist or an anarchist, as far as a lot of Americans were concerned. My mother didn't campaign for her views in public, but she did campaign for them when it came to me. She was very opposed to Senator McCarthy and quite pro-Communist, and I remember her giving me the front page of the *Milwaukee Journal* and telling me I wouldn't understand the significance then but to save it. That front page had a headline announcing the death of Joseph Stalin."

From this home with a pro-Communist atheist mother who insisted on a bar mitzvah for her son, Gerry grew into the paradox of America with its rhetoric of individual freedom and reality of racial and social oppression. "It was a striking contradiction that my parents, who were liberal about so many things, were very conservative about race," he recalls, still perplexed. "I was quite concerned by the time that I was 11 or 12 about their bigotry. Race was the first issue on which I felt they were wrong. They believed that Jewish immigrants were able to pull themselves up by hard work and community support to leave immigrant ghettos and become successful, and it was as if they felt blacks were blaming society while not demonstrating the personal, familial, and social consciousness that would allow them to escape on their own. They didn't really see that some of the problem might have something to do with society itself."

Graduating from high school in 1959, Gerry went directly off to the University of Wisconsin in Madison. He entered the university as a premed student but found new interests, too: "Madison was a hotbed of liberalism and social advocacy, and I ended up taking philosophy and psychology courses in my first year. These got me interested in psychiatry."

Gerry also joined the college fencing team and became involved in a sport that would eventually lead to membership on the Canadian fencing team and a national championship. However, he recalls those first years of the sixties as a relatively quiet time politically "except for the Cuban missile crisis and around that same time, 1962, I remember seeing a booth in the student union where some people were telling all those who would listen about American involvement in Vietnam. They talked about American military advisers in South Vietnam and handed out pamphlets that described how Americans were conspiring with the South Vietnamese to prevent legitimate elections and how dissidents were being suppressed."

Although he had been accepted for medical school after his third year of undergraduate work, Gerry completed a fourth year, partly so that he could continue with the fencing team but also because he wanted to get a degree in philosophy. "I wasn't all that politically active in college, though I was aware of the issues around Vietnam."

In 1963 he entered medical school at New York University. "That's where I first became involved with antiwar activities. Some of the professors there were quite knowledgeable about the war and organized letter-writing campaigns and brought in guest speakers, one of whom was the civil rights and antiwar lawyer William Kunstler."

Gerry was at medical school from 1963 to 1967, followed by a year of internship as a surgeon at Bellevue Hospital. While there he applied for and was granted a deferment that meant he would be allocated to one of the services, in his case the air force, but wouldn't actually have to enlist during the period of specialized study. In return he had to promise to enlist in the air force as soon as he completed his fifth year and a four-year residency. "However," Gerry says, "during my year of internship, before actually entering my residency, I realized I didn't want to spend my life doing surgery. So I decided to change specialties, which cost me my deferment. At the same time I began looking into ways to get out of the draft. Public health service was one possibility, but the deadline for applications had passed. Then I spoke with William Kunstler about applying for conscientious objector status. He asked me if I was against all wars, and I had to answer no."

There was another possibility. Gerry learned that a county hospital in El Paso, Texas, needed doctors and that the positions carried draft deferments. He applied and got a job, but a few months later, once he was in Texas, he was told by his draft board that his medical position would no longer make him eligible for deferment. Appeals were to no avail, so Gerry wrote to McGill University in Montreal: "I told them I would like to come to Canada to train in psychiatry. The university accepted me, and in the late winter or spring of 1969 I packed up and drove to Milwaukee with the idea of going to Canada.

"It was a very difficult time. I was incredibly paranoid and felt that all my movements and actions were being scrutinized. Somewhere in that drive from Texas to Milwaukee, though, I decided I couldn't go to Canada to avoid the war. I felt I wouldn't be making a political statement. It wouldn't do anything to aid the antiwar movement. I believed it would be fear more than anything else making me go to Canada, and I couldn't live with the thought that I might be a coward, even though when I had opportunities to counsel people in similar positions, I'd tell them to look at options such as going to Canada, applying for conscientious objector status, or even going to jail if they felt comfortable with that choice."

Once his decision to go to Vietnam was made, things moved quickly for Gerry. A month of basic training in San Antonio, Texas, was followed by a posting to the outpatient department at Fort Monmouth, New Jersey. After about nine months there, he was told to report to Oakland, California, for embarkation to Vietnam. "When I arrived on the West Coast, I felt as if I were a leper on death row. There was a terrible sense of anxiety. I think part of me really did believe I wouldn't be coming back. The other soldiers on the plane were very much into their own thoughts, so things were pretty quiet during the trip. As far as I could tell, most of them didn't share my opposition to the war. I expect they felt they were doing the right thing."

What Gerry remembers most about arriving at the air base in Saigon in 1970 is the smell: "It was awful. It was like stepping out of the plane and walking into an outhouse. There was a putrid, acrid smell. You could see black clouds of smoke all over the place. At first, being naive, I thought the whole fucking place had been bombed but, in fact, the stink came from burning the shitters. They poured oil in all the cans in the outhouses and burned them daily. There was also a stench from the delta clay."

The new troops, including Dr. Gerald Wiviott, were given several days of in-country training, which meant, among other things, familiarizing themselves with the enemy's favourite weapons. Gerry was then assigned to Chu Lai, one of the war's hot spots. Worse, in the field, he was detailed to Professional, which had a notorious reputation as a dangerous fire base. Professional was on a hill and had shelters built into bomb craters that were covered with corrugated tin, timbers, and dirt.

As the designated battalion surgeon, Gerry got to see the human wreckage of war up close and personal. However, he found even the daily sick call difficult. "A lot of guys didn't want to go back into the field. Skin rashes were ubiquitous. Many of the guys would rub the hell out of their skin to make the infection bigger. On the one hand, I wanted all of these guys to get out of the field so they wouldn't get killed. On the other hand, I was under pressure from the officers to keep up the field count. And I'd also hear from some of the guys in the field who'd complain if their platoons were short men. Being short meant they'd have to double up on ammo and equipment and they wouldn't have as many men for guard duty at night." For Gerry, service in Vietnam was the ultimate paradox in a life fraught with paradoxes: "I developed a tremendous sense of loyalty to the guys out in the field who were putting their lives on the line every day, while at the same time I fervently believed the whole war was fucked up and we shouldn't have been there in the first place."

Gerry was stationed at Professional for four months and then served at other fire bases for another four. "I was appropriately frightened. We were shelled all the time and occasionally Vietcong sappers would infiltrate the base. Eventually you became fatalistic and figured, If it happens, it happens. In the end, all you really cared about were your buddies."

Not surprisingly, ambivalence about the "enemy" seemed to be a way of life for many doctors in Vietnam. "Once in a while," Gerry recalls, "we would get Vietcong and North Vietnamese Army wounded. I never saw an interrogation, but I always had the feeling that even if I saved them, their interrogation would be worse than any injuries they came to me with. Intellectually I felt what we were doing to the VC and NVA was wrong, but these guys *were* the enemy and, like everybody else, I couldn't get it out of my mind that one of them might have shot someone I'd played cards with the night before."

The paradoxes for a white liberal pacifist in the American army of occupation could be found everywhere. Sometimes it seemed as if a war were going on among Gerry's fellow soldiers. "Once I tried to patch together a white artillery sergeant who'd been 'fragged' by another soldier, but he died. The sergeant had made disparaging remarks about blacks shortly before he was blown up with a grenade, so it was assumed that the fragging was a racial issue. There was a lot of friction between blacks and whites. There was some wonderful camaraderie, too, but many blacks used a hand-signal system called 'dapping' among themselves that excluded whites. That kind of tension between guys who had to count on one another out in the field just added to an already impossible situation."

Finally, after eight months in the field, twice the usual rotation, Gerry was ordered to report to the rear base hospital at Qui Nhon. "It was like Club Med with dead people," he says now, smiling wryly across from me in the comfort of his living room. "I lived in the officers' quarters and went to the officers' club for steak and lobster and good wine. Everything was cheap as hell. The PX was full of up-to-date Japanese photography and hi-fi equipment. These guys who lived in the rear were called REMFs, Rear Echelon Mother Fuckers. They lived amazingly. It was a real comfortable scene, but the work could really get to you. Once, we got 24 guys who'd been shot up in an ambush, and all the time I'd have to deal with men who'd been terribly burned or who had lost their arms or legs or both. And you never knew when to expect it. One time I saw a helmet lying on the ground near a loading zone. When I moved it, I saw someone's brains in it."

Gerry spent four months at the hospital in Qui Nhon, all the time becoming increasingly demoralized by the drinking, drugs, and sex that so many of the hospital's staff sought refuge in. After his extended period in the field, his time in Qui Nhon was something of a limbo that he was locked into while he awaited orders to be sent home. When he finally got those orders, he remembers spending a harrowing night in the barracks at Tan Son Nhut air base, waiting for the plane that would take him back to the World: "During the night, there was a huge explosion that knocked the shit out of us and threw us all out of our beds. Later I found out that a Soviet rocket had blown up the building next door. Ironically that was the closest I came to being killed in Vietnam."

The flight back to America landed in Seattle on March 1, 1971. "That was an unbelievably hard transition," Gerry says. "I don't think there's any way of adequately describing the difficulty of coming back. First of all, you feel like shit because you went there and were part of it. Second, you get real angry because nobody wants to know you. In my case, the Kent State massacre had happened the previous year and opposition to the war was probably at its height. I just remember wanting to stuff my uniform in the toilet right there in the airport. I didn't want to walk around with it on at all."

Within two days of arriving back in the United States, Gerry was given his discharge from the army. He flew to Milwaukee to stay with his parents for a time and then with his savings from Vietnam he went to Europe for a couple of months. Before leaving he applied once again to McGill's psychiatry department, and by July 1971, after returning from Europe, he was enrolled at the university.

While studying at McGill he attended a lecture given by the noted American psychiatrist Robert J. Lifton, who had just written *Home from the War*, a book examining the psychological state of soldiers returning from Vietnam. Gerry felt intense, irrational anger while listening to Lifton speak, feeling that the man had a lot of nerve to set himself up as an expert when he hadn't seen what the war was like firsthand. It was as if Lifton's talk had suddenly brought to a head all of the paradoxes, all of the conflicting feelings, all of the madness that Gerry had experienced. After the talk, Gerry spoke with Lifton, who told him that perhaps his decision to come to Canada had been a way for him to deal with the fact that, unlike many who had opposed the war, he had actually participated, so that leaving behind his native land was a kind of protest after the fact.

Gerry now works as a psychiatrist at the Allan Memorial Institute in Montreal where he specializes in couple and family therapy and lives quietly with his wife and two children. Since coming to Canada, he has been involved in various antiwar groups. In 1985 he organized the Montreal regional conference of International Physicians for the

Prevention of Nuclear War, and the success of that conference led to his co-chairing the organization's 1988 conference, something he says was "a labour of love and redemption."

When I began my interview with Gerry at eight in the evening, we both figured it would take about two hours. Now it is midnight, Gerry's wife, Paula, and his two children have long gone to sleep, and Gerry and I have consumed a couple of beers. We talk about our respective kids for a while, and Gerry proudly tells me that his oldest son, Matthew, had his bar mitzvah just a few months earlier.

I think of Gerry's strong-willed atheist mother and her rock-hard belief in justice and the need to stand up for your convictions. Paradoxes. Maybe we all have our fair share of them, but then Gerry looks at me and says, "You know, it's funny, when I came back from Vietnam, nobody wanted to listen to me about how bad things were there. The Kent State massacre had happened in 1970 while I was still in Vietnam. By the time I got back, almost everyone thought the war was wrong and they all believed it was only a matter of time before we pulled out. My whole raison d'être for going in the first place was to come back and be a more credible antiwar activist. I felt like a stranger in a strange land, and it took me quite a while to work myself out of the confusion and depression I found myself in."

Then again, maybe there aren't many other people who wrestle with the kind of paradoxes that seem to haunt Gerald Wiviott.

CHRONOLOGY

1945   Emperor Bao Dai proclaims the independence of Vietnam from France under Japanese auspices in the last months of World War II.

Germany surrenders, May 8.

Japan capitulates, August 15, after the United States drops atomic bombs on Hiroshima and Nagasaki.

Bao Dai abdicates on August 23.

Japan formally surrenders to the Allies. Ho Chi Minh declares the independence of Vietnam, September 2.

British forces under General Douglas Gracey land in Saigon on September 13 and help return authority to the French.

Lieutenant Colonel A. Peter Dewey of the oss is killed in Saigon, September 26, the first American to die in Vietnam.

Some two million Vietnamese die of famine in the north.

1946   Amid growing tensions, French warships bombard Haiphong, November 23.

Vietminh forces withdraw from Hanoi in December after attacking French garrisons. The war has begun.

1949   Bao Dai returns to Vietnam in April after three years of self-imposed exile.

1950   Ho Chi Minh declares on January 14 that the Democratic Republic of Vietnam is the only legal government. United States and Britain recognize Bao Dai's government, February 7.

On June 26 North Korea invades South Korea. President Truman, without consulting Congress, commits American troops to the war under United Nations auspices.

Truman signs legislation granting $15 million in military aid to the French for the war in Indochina, July 26.

1953   Armistice agreement signed in Korea, July 27.

1954   Battle of Dien Bien Phu begins, March 13; French defeated at Dien Bien Phu, May 7.

Bao Dai selects Ngo Dinh Diem as prime minister, June 16.

Provisional demarcation line at 17th parallel divides Vietnam. Hundreds of thousands of refugees flee from the north to the south with the help of U.S. Navy.

1955   United States begins to funnel aid directly to Saigon government in January and agrees to train South Vietnamese Army.

Ho Chi Minh, in Moscow in July, accepts Soviet aid, having earlier negotiated in Beijing for Chinese assistance.

Diem defeats Bao Dai in a referendum, October 23, and becomes chief of state; proclaims the Republic of Vietnam, with himself as president, October 26.

1959   Major Dale Buis and Sergeant Chester Ovnand killed by guerrillas at Bien Hoa on July 8, the first Americans to die in what will become the undeclared Vietnam War.

1960   John F. Kennedy defeats Richard Nixon for the presidency, November 8.

Hanoi leaders form National Liberation Front for South Vietnam, December 20, which Saigon regime dubs the Vietcong, meaning Communist Vietnamese.

1961 American-backed attempt to overthrow Fidel Castro fails at the Bay of Pigs in Cuba in April.

1962 American military assistance command formed in South Vietnam, February 6. By mid-1962 American advisers have increased from 700 to 12,000.

Kennedy forces the Soviets to withdraw missiles from Cuba in October.

1963 Duong Van Minh and other generals stage coup against Diem and Ngo Dinh Nhu, November 1; Diem and Nhu are murdered after their surrender next day. On November 22, Kennedy assassinated in Dallas; succeeded by Lyndon Johnson.

By the year's end, 15,000 American military advisers are in South Vietnam, which has received $500 million in aid during the year.

1964 North Vietnamese patrol boats attack the *Maddox,* an American destroyer in the Gulf of Tonkin, August 2. A doubtful second incident reported two days later. American aircraft bomb North Vietnam for the first time later that month. Congress passes the Gulf of Tonkin resolution on August 7, giving Johnson extraordinary power to act in Southeast Asia.

Students for a Democratic Society (SDS) begins planning first national antiwar demonstration, late December.

1965 Vietcong stage attacks against American installations, February 7. Johnson authorizes Flaming Dart, American air raids against North Vietnam. Operation Rolling Thunder, sustained American bombing of North Vietnam, begins on February 24.

Two marine battalions land to defend Da Nang airfield, March 8, the first American combat troops in Vietnam.

SDS-sponsored national antiwar demonstration in Washington, D.C., April 17.

Draft-card burning is made a crime punishable by five years in prison.

American forces defeat North Vietnamese units in the Ia Drang Valley in October, the first big conventional clash of the war.

First International Days of Protest, October 15-16.

By December, American troop strength in Vietnam reaches nearly 200,000.

1966   David Mitchell becomes the first person convicted for draft-card burning, February.

Twelve black demonstrators are arrested at a sit-in at the Atlanta, Georgia, induction centre; most are sentenced to three years in prison.

American troop strength in Vietnam reaches nearly 400,000 by year's end.

1967   Robert McNamara, U.S. secretary of defence, testifying before a Senate subcommittee in August, asserts American bombing of North Vietnam is ineffective.

In South Vietnam, Nguyen Van Thieu elected president.

Muhammad Ali is sentenced to five years in prison for refusing induction, April 28.

Communists begin major actions in September. General Westmoreland starts to fortify Khe Sanh.

National draft-card turn-in, October 16.

Joan Baez and 122 others are arrested at the Oakland, California, induction centre, October 20-22.

On October 21 more than 100,000 antiwar protesters converge on the Pentagon, vowing to shut it down or "raise" it 300 feet into the air. Norman Mailer is among demonstrators arrested.

American troop strength in Vietnam approaches 500,000 by year's end.

1968   Tet Offensive begins, January 31, as North Vietnamese and
        Vietcong attack South Vietnamese cities and towns. American
        and South Vietnamese troops recapture Hué on February 25
        after 26 days of fighting.

        On March 31, President Johnson announces partial bombing
        halt, offers talks, and says he will not run for reelection.

        Martin Luther King, Jr., assassinated, April 4.

        In one week in May, 562 Americans are killed in Vietnam.

        The Catonsville Nine (the Berrigan brothers and seven others)
        burn 378 draft records with homemade napalm in Catonsville,
        Maryland, May 17.

        Robert Kennedy assassinated, June 5.

        The Democratic National Convention in Chicago is disrupted
        by rioting, August. Among those later charged are the Chicago
        Eight (Abbie Hoffman, Jerry Rubin, Tom Hayden, Bobby Seale,
        and four others).

        Milwaukee Fourteen destroy 10,000 draft records, September.

        Richard Nixon elected president, November 5.

        Henry Kissinger chosen by Nixon as national security adviser,
        December 2.

        American troop strength in Vietnam at year's end is 540,000.

1969   Nixon begins secret bombing of Cambodia, March 18.

        Nixon proposes simultaneous withdrawal from South Vietnam
        of American and North Vietnamese forces, May 14.

        Woodstock Music Festival in Woodstock, New York, features
        Jimi Hendrix, Country Joe McDonald, Crosby, Stills, and Nash,
        Janis Joplin, and other leading lights of the era, August.

        Ho Chi Minh dies in Hanoi at age 79, September 3.

        Daniel Ellsberg begins copying Pentagon Papers, early fall.

Vietnam Moratorium and massive antiwar demonstrations in Washington, October 15.

In November, My Lai massacre revealed, which took place the year before.

American troop strength in Vietnam reduced by 60,000 by December.

1970 Fathers Daniel and Philip Berrigan go underground after destroying draft records, March.

Nixon announces, April 30, that Cambodia has been invaded by American and South Vietnamese forces.

Large antiwar protests spread across the United States. National guardsmen kill four students at Kent State University in Ohio on May 4.

Two black protesters killed at Jackson State University, May 14.

1971 U.S. invasion of Laos begins, February 8.

Weatherman bombing of U.S. Capitol building, March 1.

Lieutenant Calley convicted, March 29, of premeditated murder of South Vietnamese civilians at My Lai.

More than half a million protesters gather in Washington, D.C., for biggest antiwar demonstration yet, April 24.

New York Times begins publishing Pentagon Papers, June 13.

American troop strength in Vietnam down to 140,000 men in December.

1972 Nixon announces, January 13, withdrawal of another 70,000 troops from Vietnam, leaving 69,000 there by May.

Senator Edward Kennedy begins amnesty hearings for draft evaders, February 28.

North Vietnam launches offensive across the demilitarized zone, March 30.

On April 15, Nixon authorizes bombing of area near Hanoi and Haiphong.

North Vietnamese capture the city of Quang Tri, May 1.

Five men arrested, June 17, for breaking into Democratic National Committee offices at Watergate complex in Washington, D.C.

White House announces last U.S. ground combat troops have left Vietnam, August 12.

Nixon reelected, November 7, defeating Senator George McGovern by a landslide.

1973   Cease-fire agreements formally signed in Paris, January 27.

Last American troops leave Vietnam, March 29. Last American prisoners of war released in Hanoi, April 1.

Last military induction takes place, July 1

1974   South Vietnamese President Thieu declares in January that the war has begun again.

House Judiciary Committee votes, July 30, to recommend impeaching Nixon on three counts for attempting to cover up the Watergate affair.

Nixon resigns, August 9; replaced by Gerald Ford who, in September, announces a clemency program for draft evaders: conditional amnesty in exchange for two years' alternative service.

1975   Draft registration ends, March 29. Congress rejects Ford's request for $500 million in military aid for Thieu and South Vietnam.

In Cambodia, Phnom Penh falls to the Khmer Rouge, April 17.

Communist forces capture Saigon, April 30.

1977   On January 21, the day after his inauguration as president, Jimmy

Carter pardons most Vietnam War draft evaders.

1978   Vietnam invades Cambodia, December 25.
Thousands of "boat people" begin to flee Vietnam in December.

1979   China invades Vietnam in February.

1980   Draft registration reinstated, July 21.
Ronald Reagan elected president, November 4.

1982   Vietnam Veterans Memorial unveiled in Washington, D.C., November 11.

1985   Famine spreads in Vietnam following failure of farm collectivization program.

1986   Vietnamese Communist Party convenes in December, names Nguyen Van Linh general secretary, launches liberal economic reform program.

1988   George Bush elected president in November.

1989   Soviet leader Mikhail Gorbachev embarks on reform programs, moves toward reduced aid to Vietnam.
Collapse of communism in Eastern Europe alarms Vietnamese leaders.

1990   In September, Secretary of State James Baker meets in New York with Vietnam's Foreign Minister Nguyen Co Thach.

1991   Soviet Union ends aid to Vietnam, announces that trade will henceforth be conducted in dollars at world market prices.

Bush declares that victory in the Persian Gulf has "kicked the Vietnam syndrome."

1992   Bill Clinton elected president in November.

1994   United States ends 19-year trade embargo on Vietnam, begins to pump aid and investment into country. Vietnam and United States begin negotiations to return property to each other, including the old U.S. embassy in Saigon.

1995   Vietnam and United States sign Liaison Office Agreement, January 28. Americans open office (a quasi embassy) in Hanoi, while Vietnam opens office in Washington, D.C.

SELECTED READING

American Friends Service Committee. *The Draft?* New York: Hill and Wang, 1968.

Gitlin, Todd. *The Sixties: Years of Hope, Days of Rage.* New York: Bantam, 1987.

Herr, Michael. *Dispatches.* New York: Avon, 1978.

Karnow, Stanley. *Vietnam: A History.* Rev. ed. New York: Penguin, 1991.

Kasinsky, Renée G. *Refugees from Militarism: Draft-Age Americans in Canada.* New Brunswick, NJ: Transaction Books, 1976.

Lemm, Richard. *Prelude to the Bachannal.* Charlottetown, PEI: Ragweed, 1990.

Lifton, Robert J. *Home from the War: Vietnam Veterans – Neither Victims nor Executioners.* New York: Simon and Schuster, 1973.

Lind, Alice. *We Won't Go: Personal Accounts of War Objectors.* Boston: Beacon Press, 1968.

MacPherson, Myra. *Long Time Passing: Vietnam and the Haunted Generation.* New York: Anchor, 1984.

O'Brien, Tim. *Going After Cacciato.* New York: Dell, 1992.

——. *The Things They Carried.* New York: McClelland and Stewart, 1990.

Sibum, Norm. *Small Ceremonies.* Prince George, B C: Caitlin Press, 1978.

Powers, Thomas. *Viet Nam: The War at Home.* Boston: G. K. Hall, 1973.

Tatum, Arlo and Joseph S. Tuchinsky. *Guide to the Draft.* Boston: Beacon Press, 1969.

Wells, Tom. *The War Within: America's Battle over Vietnam.* Berkeley, C A: University of California Press, 1994.

ABOUT THE AUTHOR

ALAN HAIG-BROWN founded magazines such as *West Coast Mariner* and *West Coast Logger* in the 1980s and has written on fishing and marine affairs for a wide variety of publications, including *Professional Mariner*, *National Fisherman*, and *West Coast Fisherman*. The author of *Fishing for a Living*, a bestselling B.C. Book Award-winning account of West Coast Canadian fishing culture told through oral history and photographs, Haig-Brown now lives in New Westminster, British Columbia.